JESUS IS ENOUGH

JESUS IS
ENOUGH

Love, Hope, and Comfort
in the Storms of Life

CLAUDIA MAY

Augsburg Books
MINNEAPOLIS

JESUS IS ENOUGH
Love, Hope, and Comfort in the Storms of Life

Large-quantity purchases or custom editions of this book are available at a discount from the publisher. For more information, contact the sales department at Augsburg Fortress, Publishers, 1-800-328-4648, or write to: Sales Director, Augsburg Fortress, Publishers, P. O. Box 1209, Minneapolis, MN 55440-1209.

Scripture quotations are from the *New Revised Standard Version Bible*, copyright © 1989 by the Division of Christian Education of the National Council of the Churches of Christ in the USA. Used by permission.

Library of Congress Cataloging-in-Publication Data
May, Claudia, 1966-
  Jesus is enough : love, hope, and comfort in the storms of life / by Claudia May.
    p. cm.
  ISBN 0-8066-5117-2 (pbk. : alk. paper)
  1. Consolation. 2. Christian life. 3. Jesus Christ — Person and offices.
I. Title.

  BV4909.M387 2005
  242'.4   dc22   2005025637

Cover design by David Meyer; cover image © Doug Armand/Stone/Getty Images; book design by Michelle L. N. Cook

Manufactured in the U.S.A.

10   09   08   07   06   2   3   4   5   6   7   8   9   10

Dedicated to My Father, My Mother,

and Dougie — My Beloved Stepfather

The Reed

Its stem nests
into the silhouette
of a pregnant form
causing bruises to bloom
in the nape of its back

Worn with wear
weighed down by time
the memories of storms gone by
straddle its skin
until the peak of its blade
darkens the soil with its image

It is then the gardener
touches the single vein
running along
the arch of its back
and as he does so
it is as if a feather
finds eternal rest
in a tender breath of wind

He lays the back of his hand
under the tip of the reed
until his flesh
communes with the earth
As the reed leans toward
the flesh of his palm
his other hand
forges a shell around its body

A breeze leaks through
the lattice of his fingers
causing the reed to sway
and all the while
the hands of the gardener
shelter the reed
from the full force of the wind
and the reed remains unbroken

CONTENTS

ACKNOWLEDGMENTS

First, I want to thank Jesus for guiding me through every storm that I have encountered. Each challenging and joyous experience has made me more appreciative of his unconditional love for me. I only hope, dear Jesus, that this book is pleasing to you, and that many will experience your love in a real and tangible way.

I want to thank my family at large whose love, prayers, and support have encouraged me to become the best that I can be. I want to thank my grandparents whose vision, hard work, and sacrifice afforded our family a better life and new opportunities. It is with deep gratitude that I thank my Auntie Valerie, who I fondly call Bishop. Your love for Jesus, your sacrificial service to Grandpa, and your humble care for our family and many others both moves and inspires me.

I deeply appreciate my prayer partners, Mama Anita and Cecilia Williams, for their abounding love for Jesus and their commitment to prayer. Thank you, Mama Anita, for speaking truth into my life, especially when I do not want to receive your insights. To my dear Sister Cecilia, I am truly grateful for the times when we pondered over, grappled with, and disagreed about each other's interpretation of any number of passages of scripture. I only hope others can experience the kind of partnership in God's word that allows Jesus to have the last word.

Thank you, Curtiss, Karen, Rachel, and Jonathan DeYoung, for allowing me to be a part of your lives. I especially want to thank you, Karen, for being such an example to me of what it means to be a wife, mother, sister, and daughter. Your faithful and loving service to others embodies humility.

Thank you, Brian and Lisa Gervers, Todd and Charity Cardell, and Peter and Jessica Wholer, for providing me with a home away from home. Your prayers and generosity continue to move me.

Thank you to Greg and Sharon Miller and the Miller clan. Words cannot fully capture all that you have done for me as a family. You have been the body of Christ for me.

Thank you to my childhood friends Janine, David, Patrick, and Marcel, and all the others whose financial help enabled me to purchase my airline ticket so I could earn my doctorate in America. Most of all I want to thank you for being my friends for over twenty years. Thank you, dear Herschel, for believing in me before I could even think of believing in myself.

And to my dear friend Majella, your honesty inspires me. The countless thought-provoking conversations that we have engaged in over the years motivate me to think deeply about my relationship with Jesus and with others. Thank you for being such a great friend. And thank you, Bernadette, for your support, your wonderful friendship, and for all our incredible conversations. I have not forgotten all the ways you have come to my assistance, and I am eternally thankful.

Thank you to my Catholic brothers and sisters who serve at Pacem in Terris. Your love for Jesus and the Church has deeply shaped my faith. I especially want to thank Shirley Wanchena for her exemplary modeling out of faith.

I also want to extend my thanks to Jim Bergdoll, Mary Beth Brocklebank, Lindsey Cook, Melissa Flesner, the Folgelsons, Melanie, the Johnsons, Shelley Klevos, Tom and Evie Miller, David and Lois Murphy, Terry and Nancy Shinsato, Maureen Slattery Marsh, and the Williams for your prayers and encouragement. I especially want to thank Nina Lau Branson for her wise counsel, prayer support, and sisterhood.

I am deeply grateful for my incredible cousin Annette Taylor, who has always loved me unconditionally. She prays for me, offers me wise advice, puts Jesus first in her life, watches out for me, defends me, celebrates in my achievements, and grieves with me when I am sad. She is an exceptional woman of God who carries herself with a dignity that is birthed from the love of Jesus.

Thank you to my mentors, Dr. Margaret B. Wilkerson and Dr. Barbara T. Christian, for allowing me to learn from your wisdom, and wonderful teaching.

Thank you to my dear, dear sister Donna, who has proven to be a true friend, who supports me through all seasons of my life. I am proud to call you my sister. I am in awe of God's presence in your life, and I appreciate your humble and profound faith.

I want to thank all my teachers and brothers and sisters in Christ who have guided my love and appreciation of scripture. Anita Edwards, Nina Lau Branson, Rev. Dr. Mark Lau Branson, Rev. Dr. Greg Boyd, Rev. Anne Lau Choy, Rev. Daniel Gillquist, Rev. Darrell and Edna Geddes, Rev. Keith Johnson, Rev. Dr. David Murphy, Rev. Peggy Riley, Rev. Peter Singletary, Rev. Efrem Smith, Rev. Cecilia Williams, and Rev. Victor Waters have at different stages presented thought-provoking sermons and teachings on scripture that inspired my reflections on God's word.

Thank you to all those who gave critical feedback on my work. Michelle L. N. Cook, Nicole Benson, Rev. Dr. Mark Lau Branson, Chelsea DeArmond, and Rev. Dr. Curtiss Paul DeYoung offered invaluable comments on various stages of my draft. Thank you for your honesty and guidance. And thank you for believing in my potential as a writer and in this project.

Thank you to my students who were enrolled in the courses that I taught at the University of St. Thomas, St. Paul, Minnesota. Thank you for sharing your lives with me. I am blessed to have had the privilege of sharing a classroom of learning with you.

To Dougie, my beloved stepfather, thank you for being my cheerleader. Thank you for being proud of me. You are missed.

Thank you to Scott Tunseth, whose sound leadership helped to green light this project. Thank you to my first editor, Lois Wallentine, whose role in guiding the early stages of this book is deeply appreciated. I especially want to thank my other wonderful editor, Marcia Broucek, whose attention to detail, expertise, and consistent encouragement was insurmountable. You were God's gift to me, and I thank you for responding to his call.

Finally, I want to thank my parents for giving me life, loving me, and giving me the room to grow and make mistakes. Thank you for working to provide for me. Thank you for buying my first Bible. I thank Jesus for you, and I am profoundly blessed and truly honored to call you my mother and father.

HOPE IN THE STORM

WHAT IS ENOUGH?

What does it mean to make Jesus enough for us, in both good and bad times? Consider the story in the Gospel of Luke. When a lawyer asked Jesus what he should "do to inherit eternal life," Jesus turned the question back to him, asking him, "What is written in the law? What do you read there?" (Luke 10:26). The lawyer replied, "You shall love the LORD your God with all your heart, and with all your soul, and with all your strength, and with all your mind; and your neighbor as yourself." Jesus answered, "You have given the right answer; do this and you will live" (Luke 10:27-28).

These instructions become the checkpoints for us: Do we love the Lord our God with all our heart, soul, strength, and mind? Do we love our neighbors as ourselves? Do we want to live in the fullness of all Jesus wants us to experience in his love? Do we believe Jesus can be enough for us?

When we are seeking immediate answers to our problems, we may feel overwhelmed by such questions. We may grow despondent and struggle with feelings of inadequacy and low self-worth as we wonder whether we can follow Jesus' teachings on how we ought to live our lives. We may find that we trust Jesus in some areas of our lives more than in others. At various stages of our faith journey, we may find that just when we think we have put our trust in Jesus, an unexpected storm can reveal that we actually have placed other things and people before him.

Take heart. Hope awaits you. Jesus wants you to come to him in and out of the storms of life. Remember, when Jesus conversed with the lawyer who asked him how he could "inherit eternal life," Jesus posed questions to the lawyer and left it up to the lawyer to consider, and answer, them for himself. But the key is that the lawyer entered into a dialogue with Jesus. He listened to Jesus, he probed for answers, he sought further clarification, and Jesus did not grow impatient with him. We, too, can approach Jesus with our queries, doubts, and concerns, and he will listen to us.

Interestingly, Jesus' response to the lawyer's queries was short and to the point: "You have given the right answer; do this and you will live"; "Go and do likewise" (Luke 10:28; Luke10:37c). Jesus did not rule over the lawyer with an iron rod to see whether he would follow through on what he had gleaned. Instead, Jesus gave this lawyer the room, the time, and the space to integrate these words of wisdom into his life. In the same way, Jesus will not only patiently allow us to grow and learn from his teachings, but he will also readily shepherd us as we seek to incorporate his insights into our daily walk.

IN THE MIDST OF SUFFERING

Life's stormy trials—whether they be work-related, financial, relational, associated with domestic problems, or linked to physical or emotional ailments—can leave us feeling so distraught that our trust in Jesus fades as quickly as raindrops disappearing into the sea. Adrift in our misery, we may wonder where Jesus is during our time of trial. We may forget to seek Jesus' wisdom or stop conversing with him altogether, especially after we have prayed for a particular outcome and it appears that he has not responded to our concerns.

More commonly, a series of smaller gales rather than an enormous outburst can knock loose our foothold in faith. Failing an exam and having to take it again after working so hard to reach this threshold of our academic career, dealing with a boss who constantly micro-manages our work, battling with an insurance company who refuses to pay for our car repairs—these are just some of the smaller gales that can shake our sense of well-being and our hope in God. Shadowed by a sense of abandonment, the strain of having to address each distressing incident can make us feel as if we are trying to sop up water from the bottom of a boat with a damp handkerchief. Just as we begin to overcome an unexpected squall, fresh currents of trouble threaten to saturate our thoughts and actions.

The rise and fall of our dilemmas can leave us feeling helpless, despondent, and at times, powerless. Jesus shows us that we can cry out to God in the midst of our suffering. When he agonized over the prospect of having to confront a brutal persecution and horrific death, he never lost sight that

he was God's beloved. Even when he was nailed to the cross and cried out, "My God, my God, why have you forsaken me?" (Matthew 27:46c), Jesus still believed in God, even as he believed God had forsaken him.

Like Jesus, when we believe and abide in our core identity as beloved children of God, we, too, can withstand whatever comes our way. Jesus will guide us when we do not know which way to turn. He will love us when we feel the most unlovable. He will provide for our every need, even when we do not recognize the ways in which he upholds us.

When we weather the stormy seasons of our lives, even if we feel that Jesus has neglected us, he will continue to strengthen us. Whatever we confront, his love will never change. Permitting Jesus to love us in and through all circumstances can present us with a profound healing. Jesus is able to bring people into our lives who can offer us invaluable support, but it is Jesus who will stay awake, and will listen to us and protect us, twenty-four hours a day, seven days a week, three-hundred-and-sixty-five days a year. When we acknowledge that Jesus can restore and rejuvenate our lives, that his teachings and wisdom can sustain us in all circumstances, we will enter into a level of peace that we have never known before.

Nonetheless, learning to make Jesus a priority is a lifelong process of discovery. Consider the story of Peter. After the Last Supper, and after Jesus and the disciples "went out to the Mount of Olives," Jesus revealed to his disciples that he would be persecuted, killed, then raised from the dead. Peter and the other disciples adamantly insisted that they would never disown or abandon him (Matthew 26:30-35).

Yet in the dark of night, when guards took Jesus into custody and bystanders asked Peter if he was with Jesus, Peter denied ever knowing Jesus—three times (Matthew 26:69-75). Later, the resurrected Jesus asked Peter three times whether he loved him, and each time Peter declared his devotion to Jesus (John 21:15-19). With each question, Peter was given the opportunity to consider the extent to which Jesus was enough for him, and with each question Peter articulated that he would surrender all of himself to Jesus' will.

In our lives as well, honest introspection can make us consider our love for Jesus. These moments of reflection can also provide us with another opportunity to deepen our commitment to him, as Peter did.

THE GREAT LOVE OF OUR LIVES

So be encouraged. When our solo attempts to solve our problems fail, when we begin to realize that our own efforts are not enough, and the resources and people we have become reliant upon cannot completely eradicate our concerns, we may come to a new awareness that Jesus is there for us. In the womb of our storms, we can discover that Jesus is there to be our comfort, the great love of our lives. He can be our refuge in and out of strife. Hope in him can save us from being swept away by the torrents of hard times.

Jesus not only promises that he will stand by us, but his relationship with his heavenly Father offers us the key to responding to hardship: God is enough for Jesus. No matter what Jesus encounters, he knows where he comes from: He is born out of God's love. He knows where he is going: He will reside in the love of his heavenly Father for eternity. Jesus promises us that we, too, will never be separated from this love:

> *"As the Father has loved me, so I have loved you; abide in my love. If you keep my commandments, you will abide in my love, just as I have kept my Father's commandments and abide in his love. I have said these things to you so that my joy may be in you, and that your joy may be complete."(John 15:9-11)*

The Greek root word for abide is *meno,* which also means "to remain." If we remain in the love of Jesus daily, we will discover God's care for us and experience the comfort of God's love. We no longer have to feel as if we do not belong to anyone or anything. When we truly rest in the knowledge of what Jesus has done for us, his presence will constantly inhabit our lives, and we will be rooted in the assurance that we belong to God. Just like Jesus, we can say, "I know where I have come from and where I am going" (John 8:14c). Jesus is our home. He is the great love of our lives. In him we find shelter from the storm. In him we have hope, contentment, and an eternal resting place. This will not prevent trials or traumas or troubling emotions from marking our lives, but through it all, Jesus' love enables us to triumph over these tribulations.

JESUS, THE STORYTELLER

Throughout the course of his ministry, Jesus used stories to give insight into his teachings, and his stories continue to speak to the far-reaching scope of our human experiences. Following Jesus' example, I introduce each chapter in this book with a story that provides insight on how a particular emotional storm influences us. Some of these stories come from my own life or from experiences that friends have shared with me. Other stories are written as short fictional narratives. Each chapter also includes a brief narrative enactment of a biblical scene. Written in creative prose, these renditions of biblical passages flesh out some of the key themes inherent in the text. These creative segments are not meant to replace God's words or even to add to them, but they are intended to engage your pondering on the human dimensions of these biblical stories.

The scripture passages highlighted in this work explore how Jesus responds to various trials. While this book mainly focuses on Gospel narratives dealing with a particular storm of life, some entries incorporate insights from other areas of the New Testament, as well as verses from the Old Testament, just as Jesus references the Hebrew scriptures in his teachings. A short prayer closes the end of each daily reflection, and at the end of the chapter, there is a list of practical guidelines for dealing with a specific trial.

Ultimately, this book aims to be a contemplative aid that sheds some light on how to reflect on scripture and apply its teachings to everyday life. Taking time to muse upon God's word can sometimes feel like one more task to add to your busy life. But it may well be that, during the more turbulent seasons of your life, scripture will become more meaningful, vibrant, and relevant. Whatever state of mind you are in, Jesus' love is waiting for you; his love beckons you to find strength in his wisdom.

MY STORY

My own journey of experiencing the life-giving properties of scripture has not been without its ups and downs. For the longest time, I saw the Bible as a nice book to look at, especially when each page was edged in fine gold. But if I wanted to curl up in my armchair, drink a cup of tea, and read a good book, the Bible would not have been my first choice.

I knew snatches of Jesus' life story. I was acquainted with the narratives that told of his birth, familiar with his performance of a few miracles, and aware of his death and resurrection, but I had never read any of the Gospels fully. Still, when I was a graduate student in pursuit of my Ph.D., I had the audacity to join a parables covenant group whose mission centered on formulating Bible studies for our congregation. This covenant group also partnered with our pastor to select the biblical texts and themes to include in his preaching. Needless to say, any suggestions I made were based on my opinion since, more often than not, I failed to diligently pore over the text for our studies. On those rare occasions when I did scan scripture, it did not occur to me to ask Jesus what he wanted me to learn from his words.

Thankfully, Jesus smiled on me. He was patient. He did not pester or rush me to apply his words to my life. He just waited for me to come to him. Our parables covenant group, along with members of our children's covenant group and other volunteers, organized Wednesday soup-and-Bible-study nights. After sharing a meal together, we read, reflected on, and discussed a passage of scripture together. Slowly, these gatherings began to motivate me to spend more time reading the Bible. My receptiveness to scripture soon evolved to the point where my desire to know more about Jesus grew.

But it was not just the reading of scripture that liberated me. It was the realization that its words are relevant to my life. I became enamored with the human struggles, challenges, joys, and sorrows dominating the pages of the Bible. I discovered that my emotions are legitimated in scripture. I began to deeply appreciate that the Bible does not shy away from the messiness of our humanity—our day-to-day struggles, the complexity of our personas, the unpredictability of our moods, the endearing and non-endearing aspects of our character. Just like many of the characters in the Bible, we are not always loving, kind, generous, and thoughtful. We get angry, we worry, and we struggle with doubt, fear, jealousy, and unforgiveness. Sometimes we love Jesus, and other times we do not know what to feel about him. We are full of wonderful yet exasperating human contradictions, and still, Jesus loves us.

Even though my study of the Bible has been largely affirming and brought much healing into my life, there are seasons when the prospect of reading scripture does not imbue me with a sense of euphoria. Sometimes it's the last thing I want to do. During these particular desert seasons, I debate with Jesus, present my worries, share with him my anger about his teachings, and am humbled when I discover he is right. Amid all my struggles, and regardless of how long I have been a Christian, I am learning that my choice to follow Jesus, even when I do not have answers to the questions I ask of him, is a decision I choose to make daily. Through it all, I pray and call upon Jesus to renew my passion for his word. I have never sensed Jesus dismissing my concerns, but I have felt his delight as I bring all that I am to him.

Jesus is teaching me that even though I may not realize the immediate advantages of reading scripture, the long-term benefits are immeasurable. My times of meditating on scripture may not always feel all inspiring, but just as I need food to live, and air to breathe, so I need the word of God to experience the love of Jesus. I have since discovered that my more fruitful times of reading scripture have filled me with a storehouse of knowledge and wisdom and stories that I can call upon, and be encouraged by, when I am spiritually depleted by the adversities of life.

MY PRAYER FOR YOU

Jesus does not intend for us to walk this faith journey alone. He wants us to be intimately connected with a wider body of believers who will support, challenge, and nurture us through our seasons of life. Our friends, families, and colleagues, as well as our church leaders and brothers and sisters in Christ, can offer us great support. Yet they may not always be able to soothe away the emotional storms from our lives.

When the circumstances around you do not change as quickly as you'd like, when stormy emotions infiltrate your thoughts, take heart. For as you abide in Jesus and he abides in you, and as you learn to rest in his arms and tell him all about your troubles, as you listen to him and see his presence in your life, you will be calmed by his gentle touch. By allowing Jesus to love you through his words, your understanding and experience of these storms can and will change.

I pray you will be inspired to ask Jesus to help you experience scripture in new ways so that your faith and understanding of his love will flourish. If your passion for God's word has been rekindled or deepened, I will be extremely thankful to Jesus for his guidance, because there is no other teacher like Jesus. Amen.

> "Everyone then who hears these words of mine and acts on them will be like a wise man who built his house on rock. The rain fell, the floods came, and the winds blew and beat on that house, but it did not fall, because it had been founded on rock. And everyone who hears these words of mine and does not act on them will be like a foolish man who built his house on sand. The rain fell, and the floods came, and the winds blew and beat against that house, and it fell — and great was its fall!"
>
> Now when Jesus had finished saying these things, the crowds were astounded at his teaching, for he taught them as one having authority, and not as their scribes. (Matthew 7:24-29)

1. STRESS

As soon as I closed the door to my one room hermitage and sat in my rocking chair overlooking a forest area, a deep, uninterrupted peace enveloped me. Here in the cavern of this hermitage I rested, shutting out all distractions and letting the busyness of my life pass me by. This divine rest was like residing in a safe house while the torrents of life continued to rage, rain lashed against the windows, and wind beat against its exterior, but inside, I was secure in a house as solid as a rock.

On this particular silent retreat, I had not seen anyone for two days, yet loneliness found no room in my heart. As I prepared to leave my cabin for the last time, I sensed Jesus prompting me to set aside my journal and take a walk with him. I admit I protested a little, but I heeded Jesus' words, although reluctantly, and made my way toward the woods.

The branches of the trees seemed to raise their limbs in adoration to their Creator. A breeze fanned my face and threaded through my hair. I did not know the names of the birds whose song joined in this serenade of nature, but the peaks and valleys of their song sounded like a lullaby. Bordering the ledge of the pathway sat small white flowers raising their faces to the sky. Then I sensed his voice: "You see that flower over there? I created that for you . . . and that one and that one and that one . . ."

It is as if Jesus had handed me an exquisite bouquet of flowers. This was the world that God made, and my Creator wanted me to rejoice in the magnificence of this expression of love. I breathed in the fragrance of love and exhaled a breath of praise.

Along the way, I noticed a reed standing by the banks of the lake. Clearly battered by the elements and bent by the erratic shifts of the wind, this fragile but resilient reed somehow reminded me of myself. Until embarking on this retreat, I had been worn out and bruised by a series of unexpected stormy events in my life. So when I observed this single reed, still standing against the elements, the verse from Isaiah 42:3 came to my mind: "a bruised reed he will not break." Now basking in the glory

of God's creation, I was reminded of God's tender care for that bruised reed, and for me.

As I continued my hike, I smiled because Jesus knows me well. If I had brought my journal with me, I would have busily written down all that I observed. My expectation of what I "should" notice would have numbed me to the things Jesus wanted me to feel, blinded me to the things he wanted me to see, and deafened me to the things he wanted me to hear. I would have paid little to no attention to the small, seemingly insignificant timbres and sights of God's creation. With no distractions, I could accept this gift of love. Later on it occurred to me that whenever I felt overwhelmed by life, I could look into my heart and recall this moment.

For many of us, such periods of tranquility are rare. Do you feel tired? Drained? Burnt out? Exhausted? Fed up? Does your busy lifestyle keep you from dealing with the more important matters in your life? Do the demands of your life feel overwhelming? Perhaps you are finding it difficult to cope with an ever-growing number of problems.

You are not alone.

The symptoms of stress might emerge in a physical way: a slow heartburn that never seems to fully go away, a throbbing headache, a racing heartbeat, nausea, a persistent neck strain, loss of appetite——or the opposite. Some of us might find that we have become reliant on certain behaviors to get us through the day. We may go overboard at work, keep our schedules teeming with appointments, overeat or overspend, drink more alcohol, become dependent on medications or drugs, or escape through movies, television, shopping, gambling, the Internet, or sex——all to keep ourselves preoccupied.

Stress creates stress; it creates situations where we feel unable to let go. We may believe our business cannot function without our guidance. The needs of our friends, families, and colleagues may seem so pressing that we feel we cannot possibly step back. We may feel that our problems will continue to grow if we are not constantly present and attentive to them. Maybe you find it difficult to cut back on commitments because you think you will lose your job, your social standing, your financial sense of well-being, or other people's approval.

Jesus gives us a very important clue about how to handle stress. And yet it is easy to miss or pass over those sections of scripture documenting Jesus' custom to go to a quiet place to spend time with God. Oftentimes, these sparse comments are sandwiched between passages charting his magnificent teachings and healing ministry. We are told little about what Jesus did when he went away. Still, it is clear that these times of solitude were a significant priority for him and a key component of his relationship with God. It was not the *doing* of ministry but the *being*, the *abiding* in the love of God that underscored these times apart.

But many of us have never learned the importance that Jesus placed on going away to a solitary place to be with God. Many of us have not been exposed to people who have modeled this essential feature of Jesus' ministry. Then there are those of us who feel too overwhelmed by life to even consider carving out time to pray. Or, when we do tell Jesus about our concerns, we are reluctant to trust that he can really help us. We still feel as if we need to handle our dilemmas ourselves.

Again it is helpful to consider how Jesus responded to the demands placed upon him. Jesus embraced the importance of seeking out God's wisdom through prayer. This time was essential not only to Jesus' sense of well-being, but it sustained him in everything he did. By example, Jesus gives us the foundation for handling stress, and provides us with strategies for renewing our energy by showing us how to stay in relationship with God.

Give yourself a few minutes to picture Jesus
at early morning prayer:

*In the morning, while it was still very dark, he got up
and went to a deserted place, and there he prayed. (Mark 1:35)*

Night veils the sky; stars speckle its vast canvas. Birds have yet to raise their song to the heavens, and the bright shades of morning have yet to cast light onto the rugged terrain. While the hues of night are still divorced from the first flickers of daybreak, Jesus rises from his sleep and journeys to a deserted place to pray.

A peaceful lull surrounds him as he steps into the quietness of the morning night. As he breathes in the crisp air, the only footsteps heard are his own. Love embraces him as the call of his heavenly Father beckons. Encircled by the peaceful setting, they are alone. The poor and the needy, the sick and the emotionally wounded do not crowd this isolated terrain. The foliage marking the ground, and the clouds roaming the dense morning light stand as witnesses to this meeting between a Father and his Son.

As Jesus voices words of adoration to his Father and declares words of thanksgiving, his prayers of reverence mesh with the delicate hush of the wind. Only his Father hears the petitions of his heart. And as stillness covers them, Father and Son converse into the dawn of the morning light until the full bloom of the sun basks them in warmth, and the birds proclaim the coming of a new day with their symphony of praise.

SEEKING SOLITUDE

The apostles gathered around Jesus, and told him all that they had done and taught. He said to them, "Come away to a deserted place all by yourselves and rest a while." (Mark 6:30)

Jesus and the disciples probably gathered often to share stories about what they had seen and done. We can imagine them laughing, crying, and arguing. The disciples were likely eager to tell Jesus how his teachings enabled them to heal the sick, serve the poor, and care for those in need—as well as voice their frustrations about daily tribulations. Jesus listened to their stories and gave them his undivided attention. In fact, we are told they "told him *all* that they had done and taught."

But Jesus did one other thing as well: He lovingly instructed them to go to a deserted place where they would not be distracted by or focused on the needs of others. In this lonely place, they could slow down, allow Jesus' peace to nestle in their minds, and rest in the warmth of God's love.

We need to take this point to heart: Jesus *wanted* his disciples to take some time off from their duties. He not only gave them permission to seek solitude, he *commanded* them to do so. He was aware how their energy could be taxed by the demands of others. In his fathomless love for his disciples, he taught them to be mindful of taking care of their minds, bodies, and souls. And in the timing of his invitation, Jesus encouraged them not to wait until they got to the place of exhaustion before taking some time away.

We live in a world where our identities and self-esteem are all too often intertwined with our accomplishments. Our fast-paced lives can make carving out times of solitude seem like a form of idleness. So when Jesus tells us to rest, his instruction is refreshingly countercultural.

Give yourself permission to seek solitude and rest. You do not always need to be doing something. Don't wait until you are completely depleted of energy before acting upon Jesus' invitation to "come away to a deserted place all by [yourself] and rest a while."

PRAYER

Jesus, teach me how to cultivate a lifestyle that enables me to trust you with the demands of everyday life so that I can take time to be alone with you. Amen.

THE VALUE OF REST

For many were coming and going, and they had no leisure even to eat. And they went away in the boat to a deserted place by themselves. (Mark 6:31b-32)

The steady stream of visitors traveling to see Jesus—and the constant demands people made on his disciples—meant that there were periods when they had little time even to eat. We are not told whether the disciples resented the push and pull of the crowd, but we do know that Jesus was mindful. He knew his disciples could not sustain their efforts to care for others if they were not able to find enough moments to replenish their bodies with food or get time to rest. Also, Jesus was aware that few, if any, of the individuals who gathered daily to see him would consider the welfare of his disciples. With this in mind, Jesus knew it was important for his family of disciples to spend time away together.

It is easy to ignore our need to take care of ourselves, even when things are going well. But when the demands of life seem to occupy our every waking moment, when the wants of others overwhelm us, we may be especially susceptible to putting our own needs for food and rest in jeopardy. Our well-intentioned actions may not only end up hurting us, but will have an effect on those close to us as well. If we consistently put the needs of others before our own families, or let outside commitments make us less attentive to our family's wants, resentment may brew within our relational circles. Family members may even act out in destructive ways because they believe this is the only way they can get our attention.

Perhaps you are not eating well, not getting enough rest, or not connecting with family members or trusted friends. Perhaps you are ignoring your personal needs. This passage from the Gospel of Mark invites you to heed Jesus' advice.

Sometimes giving yourself permission to rest is one of the more difficult steps to take when following Jesus. If this is something you struggle with, Jesus is more than happy to teach you how to abide in his peace. Ask him to show you how to develop a lifestyle that values rest. Hear his welcoming words: "Come to me, all you that are weary and are carrying heavy burdens, and I will give you rest. Take my yoke upon you, and learn from

me; for I am gentle and humble in heart, and you will find rest for your souls. For my yoke is easy, and my burden is light" (Matthew 11:28-30).

PRAYER

Jesus, I confess that I sometimes find it difficult to take the time to rest. Help me to be sensitive to your leading when I need to let go of some responsibilities, or reorder my priorities, so I can get the rest I need. Amen.

A BALANCING ACT

And they went away in the boat to a deserted place by themselves. Now many saw them going and recognized them, and they hurried there on foot from all the towns and arrived ahead of them. As he went ashore, he saw a great crowd; and he had compassion for them, because they were like sheep without a shepherd; and he began to teach them many things. (Mark 6:32-34)

Have you ever tried to take some time off for yourself, but someone kept asking for your assistance with a problem? Jesus and his disciples faced this dilemma because they could not go anywhere without being recognized. As soon as they tried to go off by themselves to rest, people noticed that they had departed, and the crowds traveled on foot from the surrounding towns to arrive at their destination ahead of them. The scriptures do not reveal how the disciples reacted when they saw people waiting for them on the shoreline. Scripture does emphasize, however, that Jesus took center stage as he, and not the disciples, responded to the people eagerly awaiting their arrival. It was Jesus who stepped out of the boat and greeted the crowd. It was Jesus who had compassion for them and taught them "many things." And it was Jesus who gave the disciples the time and space to eat, to enjoy each other's company, and to rest without interruption.

Jesus' decision relieved his disciples of the burden of feeling as if they had to always be aware of the needs of others. You, too, can take great comfort in the knowledge that you do not have to strive to be everything to everybody. There will be periods when Jesus will steer you away from the pressures of everyday life. He may bring someone or a group of people to partner with you as you deal with a stressful circumstance. He may eliminate the issue you face. Ultimately, Jesus will always intercede on your behalf. The question is, how willing are you to let Jesus take care of you? It takes humility to know you cannot cope with all the stressful predicaments you bear. It takes humility to admit that you do not have all the answers.

Begin by asking yourself, "Do I really trust Jesus to handle my challenges?" Then ask Jesus to teach you the "many things" you need to learn about replenishment.

PRAYER

Jesus, help me trust you when I face tribulations that would divert me from taking care of my body, mind, and spirit. Help me balance my giving with my receiving, and give me the wisdom of your discernment. Amen.

A PARENTING LESSON

In the morning, while it was still very dark, he got up and went out to a deserted place, and there he prayed. (Mark 1:35)

After teaching in the synagogue, Jesus visited the home of his disciples Simon and Andrew. When they told him that Simon's mother-in-law was struck with a fever, he healed her. Then "that evening, at sundown, they brought to him all who were sick or possessed with demons. And the whole city was gathered around the door. And he cured many who were sick with various diseases, and cast out many demons" (Mark 1:32-34a).

It would be an understatement to say that Jesus was a busy man and very much in demand. The "whole city" congregated around the door of Simon's house! Men, women, children, young and old, people from all walks of life realized their absolute need for Jesus. And in response, the disciples brought all these people to Jesus, and he turned no one away. He did not complain. He did not grumble. He just took care of everyone who came to him. When he was done, he could have stuck around to receive accolades or waited to be congratulated for the miracles he had performed. Instead, in the early call of morning, "he got up and went to a deserted place, and there he prayed."

It is interesting to note that Jesus often took these spiritual excursions after he performed many miracles. This suggests that Jesus did not need to simply "get away," but rather that his mission and purpose in life were sustained by these times of close communion with God. Away from the hordes who followed him, Jesus could receive the love, comfort, and wisdom of his Father. It was a significant time of fellowship when his Father could parent him.

There is much to learn from Jesus in this regard. No matter how demanding your work is, or how much good you are doing, don't forget that God, through Jesus Christ, wants to minister to you, nurse your wounds, and parent you, also. When you pray, you, too, can experience God's loving kindness and tender care.

PRAYER

Jesus, show me how I can experience the care of my heavenly Father. Amen.

SETTING PRIORITIES

And Simon and his companions hunted for him. When they found him, they said to him, "Everyone is searching for you." (Mark 1:36-37)

At some point while Jesus was off spending time in prayer, his disciples began to miss him, so they initiated a search. Although Jesus placed a high premium on spending alone time with his heavenly Father, he did not hide in a place where he could not be reached. And Simon and his companions were persistent; they did not stop their quest until they came face to face with Jesus. But they were not alone, for the throng who had gathered outside Simon's house had also been searching for him. Such was their desire to be near Jesus, their want for his healing touch, their hunger for his teaching.

The relevance of Jesus—his teachings, his wisdom, and his love   can be crowded out by the din of this world. Demands, obligations, responsibilities, and people vie for your attention. You can be bombarded with information and advice telling you what you should and should not do. Searching for Jesus can be less of a priority when you are confronted with so many opinions that tell you how you ought to live your life.

How would your life change if you made Jesus a priority? The stress-reducing benefits of seeking Jesus are limitless. In him you can find rest and wise counsel. In him you can find the strength to confront the struggles you are up against. Just as Jesus made God his priority, so you can live a less pressure-filled life when you put Jesus first.

PRAYER

Jesus, help me to hunger for your presence. Deepen my awareness of your desire to meet my every need. Help me to make you a priority in my life. Amen.

STAYING FOCUSED

"Let us go on to the neighboring towns, so that I may proclaim the message there also; for that is what I came out to do." And he went throughout Galilee, proclaiming the message in their synagogues and casting out demons. (Mark 1:38-39)

When Simon and his friends found Jesus, he did not say that he was too tired or that he had already done his share. He did not tell them it was his day off and that they shouldn't bother him. On the contrary, Jesus wanted to move on to the next town so he could continue his work.

Despite the never-ending requests for help and healing, and despite knowing there were even more obstacles and hardships ahead, Jesus kept pressing forward. The time between tasks that Jesus spent in solitude with God refreshed him, gave him perspective, and guided his next step. Jesus shared with his disciples "for I have not spoken on my own, but the Father who sent me has himself given me a commandment about what to say and what to speak. And I know that his commandment is eternal life. What I speak, therefore, I speak just as the Father has told me" (John 12:49-50). Jesus knew what he came to do.

When you feel pressured on all sides, it is easy to lose focus of what you are doing, what direction God wants you to be moving. You may end up trying to please others instead of following God's commission. You may rely too much on others' opinions, giving them the power to define you and shape your self-worth. But God holds a purpose and vision for you that can lift you above the "push and pull" of everyone's opinion.

If you are not sure what God's purpose for you is, ask Jesus to clarify your calling. And then ask Jesus to help you make choices that will keep you focused. When you stay centered on your calling, you will not be distracted or pulled away by the crowds' activities or preoccupations. If you look to Jesus' example and seek to embody God's purpose for you, you can remove yourself from the stress of having to please others.

PRAYER

Jesus, help me not to be swayed by the opinions of others, but to seek out your guidance on where I ought to go and what you want me to do. Amen.

SITTING WITH JESUS

A large crowd kept following [Jesus], because they saw the signs that he was doing for the sick. Jesus went up the mountain and sat down there with his disciples. (John 6:2-3)

Everywhere Jesus went, the crowds seemed to follow, and Jesus responded to their needs. But we are also told that, at times, Jesus withdrew from the crowds and went to a private place with his disciples. The scriptures do not specify what Jesus did when he went to the mountain; he is described as simply sitting. This unassuming posture may speak to how much Jesus enjoyed the company of his disciples, but it also illustrates that Jesus did not always need to be actively engaged in the *doing* of ministry to fulfill his purpose. He did not have to keep *doing* to impress his followers.

It is often a good idea in our faith journey to think about whether our motives are fueled by a genuine desire to follow Jesus or to impress others. If our desire to serve is motivated by how others will perceive us, we end up being driven by performance, and we amplify the stress in our lives. When we place our self-worth in the hands of others, it is like attempting to fill a bottomless well with water. We can keep on pouring our time and energy into looking for the approval of others, but it never seems to be enough. As a result, the level of stress and fatigue in our lives grows as we try to ignore the dull sense of unfulfillment shadowing our lives and sapping us of energy.

There is much to learn from Jesus in this story. Just as Jesus did not focus on what others are doing or not doing, Jesus does not want you to be bound by the opinions and agendas of others. Remember, Jesus sat with his disciples and was happy to be with them. They were content in his presence. If you are feeling stressed out from work, weighed down by family matters, or just deluged by life in general, take this to heart: It is enough to sit with Jesus.

PRAYER

Jesus, help me to find contentment in your presence. And reveal to me when my acts of service are motivated by factors other than glorifying your name. Amen.

WHO ARE YOU?

Jesus realized that they were about to come and take him by force to make him king. (John 6:15a)

Evening began to mask the day, and Jesus' followers were hungry. Many had traveled great distances to be with Jesus, yet they had not thought to bring any food. So when Jesus arranged to feed them, they readily accepted his gift of hospitality. Jesus successfully provided a meal for five thousand people by multiplying five barley loaves and two fish offered by a little boy. The people ate "as much as they wanted" (John 6:11). There was more than enough food to go around, and the people were full and satisfied. After they finished eating, Jesus instructed the disciples to "gather up the fragments left over, so that nothing may be lost" (John 6:12b). The disciples placed the leftovers in twelve buckets, and each container was filled to the brim.

The crowd was so in awe of Jesus' latest miracle that they announced he "is indeed the prophet who is to come into the world" (John 6:14b). In their zeal, and quite possibly appreciation of Jesus, they aimed to crown him king. They never asked Jesus whether he wanted to receive such a title, yet they must have instinctively known that Jesus would not willingly embrace it, because they decided to take him by force. We can understand the crowd's desire to show their gratitude to Jesus. The irony is that, by trying to honor Jesus, the crowd dishonored him because they attempted to force him to accept an identity that they had constructed for him.

The stress of being caught up in a crowd mentality is readily apparent in our society, from feeling pressured to buy certain products to being so swept away by the home team's win that normally nonviolent people erupt in destructive behavior. Have you ever been in a predicament where you felt as if you were being swept away by the beliefs or perspectives of others? Have you ever found yourself wanting to speak up when someone voiced a strong opinion but were afraid to go against the tide of their convictions? Have you ever felt pressure to be someone you're not? Consider for a moment that the scripture begins with the phrase "Jesus realized . . ."

The next time you feel stressed by the need to live up to other people's expectations, forced roles, and unexamined beliefs, ask Jesus to help you realize what he wants you to do and become in him.

PRAYER

Jesus, help me not to be led, or to lead others, into making choices that do not honor you. Help me to be the person you created me to be. Amen.

BUILDING A RELATIONSHIP

He withdrew again to the mountain by himself. (John 6:15b)

When the crowd wanted to make Jesus a king, his response was a simple one: He withdrew *again* to the mountain by himself. Regardless of the demands placed on his time and energies, Jesus continued to nurture these times with God. It was God's wisdom and not the perspective of others that guided his decisions and actions. Day by day, moment by moment, he depended on God. His steady resolve, his focus on doing God's will, and his sense of contentment stemmed from his understanding that God loved him like no other. And only God's strength could uphold him when he faced the challenges of ministry.

Taking the time to spend periods of solitude with God was not a one-time event for Jesus. He withdrew again and again and again, and his determination to do so was essential to his ability to love and care for others. This is a message and a lesson in dealing with the pressures of life that we cannot hear enough. Every day we are constantly bombarded with responsibilities, meetings, and plans that can keep us from being present to Jesus. This is precisely when we need to follow in Jesus' footsteps: Our times of solitude need to be more than one-time events.

Jesus is your friend, your brother, your Lord, and your companion through all trials, but building a relationship with Jesus, and learning to rely on his wisdom, takes time. Scheduling periodic retreats where you can spend intervals of solitude with Jesus is essential if you are to be less ruled by stress. In the quiet of his presence, you can be fully attentive to what Jesus has to say to you. In the tenderness of his presence, you can be embraced by his reassurance that you are not alone. In the fullness of his presence, you can experience again and again his sustaining love.

PRAYER

Jesus, help me to adopt the practice of making time for you in my daily schedule so that I can find peace and hope in your presence. Replenish my need for you. Amen.

THERE IS HOPE

Now when all the people were baptized, and when Jesus also had been baptized and was praying, the heaven was opened. (Luke 3:21)

In the scriptures, Jesus is described as being tempted in every way, but he remained without sin. So why did Jesus allow John the Baptist to baptize him? Even John the Baptist declared to the crowd, "I baptize you with water; but one who is more powerful than I is coming; I am not worthy to untie the thong of his sandals. He will baptize you with the Holy Spirit and fire" (Luke 3:16). Still, despite John's humble admissions, Jesus asked John to baptize him. In receiving this spiritual sacrament, Jesus demonstrated his understanding of our human condition.

In his desire to connect with humanity, Jesus participated in experiences intended to draw us closer to God. Jesus' actions reflect a God who wants to demonstrate an everlasting love that forgives all our sins. It is a love that cleanses and transforms every aspect of our lives. Sin adds stress to our lives and deprives us of peace. But there is hope. Jesus empathizes with our struggles. He reaches out to us even when we sin against him: "For we do not have a high priest who is unable to sympathize with our weaknesses, but we have one who in every respect has been tested as we are, yet without sin. Let us therefore approach the throne of grace with boldness, so that we may receive mercy and find grace to help in time of need" (Hebrews 4:15-16).

When the stress of "not living up"—not living up to friends' expectations, your colleagues' criterion, your neighbors' or even your own standards—accumulates, you have an unlimited source of encouragement. Jesus' love does not keep score. As you surrender your sins to Jesus, you can know that there is no end to his ability to forgive.

PRAYER

Jesus, thank you for loving me even when I struggle with sin. Help me to know that I am valuable in your sight and that your forgiveness always invites me into your love. Amen.

EXPERIENCING ACCEPTANCE

The Holy Spirit descended upon him in bodily form like a dove. And a voice came from heaven, "You are my Son, the Beloved; with you I am well pleased." (Luke 3:22)

After Jesus was baptized, he prayed, and God heard his words of adoration. We do not know what Jesus said, but the heavens opened up, the Holy Spirit descended upon him like a dove, and God voiced his love for Jesus by calling him Beloved.

It is significant that God expressed this proclamation of love *before* Jesus entered into full-time ministry. Jesus had not yet conducted any of the miracles and healings that he would be known for, and still God showered him with love. God's pleasure in him was not dependent on what Jesus had done or would do, but emerged out of a love that proclaimed who Jesus was called to be: God's Beloved Son.

We live in a world where our identity can be defined by what we do for a living, what we earn, where we live, who we know, or what we wear. It is a world that tells us we will never be quite good enough. No matter how hard we try, our world encourages us to work harder and longer hours to prove ourselves, to justify our worth over and over again. The yardsticks that we measure our lives by can become the ideals we pursue and the standards we endeavor to meet. We may chase after a lifestyle that places us in debt. Our constant seeking of approval may create stress on a day-to-day basis. In the midst of these pressures, the simple truth that God loves us unconditionally can get lost.

Do you know what it is like to be loved by someone who loves you for who you are, rather than what you can do for them? What if you cannot afford to buy a house or purchase a car or keep up with the latest fashions? What if you did not get the promotion you badly wanted? It is comforting to know that Jesus will not treat you as a failure if you do not acquire the titles or living standards that others say you should aspire to attain. Jesus simply waits for you to come to him. Just as God loved him *before* he started his ministry, so Jesus will love and accept you. Jesus

promised, "I have said these things to you so that my joy may be in you, and that your joy may be complete" (John 15:11).

Will you allow Jesus' love and acceptance to be enough for you?

PRAYER

Jesus, help me to be honest with you about the ways in which I put other people and my desire for other things before you. Teach me how to be dependent on you for my self-worth and identity so I can freely live in your love. Amen.

MANAGING STRESS

The following guidelines offer some ways to live a life less ruled by stress. Whatever strategies you decide to employ, I pray you will find solace in Jesus' teachings, and allow him to lead you into a lifestyle clothed in peace and joy.

1. Ask Jesus to help you rest in him. *If you find that stress lines your daily thoughts and marks your nightly sleep, ask Jesus to help you find rest in his presence.*

The custom of going away to a quiet place was an essential part of Jesus' relationship with God. These retreats re-fueled Jesus' energy and gave him a much-needed boost to continue in the challenges of ministry. Like Jesus, you can go to a place where you are less distracted by the demands of life. Like Jesus, you can realize the benefits of devoting a measure of your day to God.

Think about creating a space in your home where there is an atmosphere of calm. Line a wall with a few choice scriptures, place candles in the room to represent the light of Jesus, or put a cross in the room to remind you of Jesus' sacrificial love. When you enter this room, ask Jesus to encircle you with his peace. You can read, journal, pray, or be still and not say a word.

Maybe you can get up earlier than others in your household for a precious time of solitude with Jesus. You might read a portion of scripture and settle into this period by being open to reflection and communication with God. Surrender any expectations you may have about what you will learn and what Jesus will teach you during these moments together. Let yourself be in the moment. If you don't happen to be an early morning person, but you are finding it difficult to find another part of the day to be with Jesus, ask him to help you get up before your usual hour so you can have some time with him.

The most important thing is to carve out space and time to be with Jesus. If you cannot do this in your home, perhaps you can go to a favorite park and sit by the lake, take a walk in your neighborhood, or spend your lunch hour with Jesus. Maybe you can sit in your church sanctuary when there are no activities going on. You might spend a couple of days at a

retreat center or visit a monastery for a couple of hours. Or go hiking in a wooded area or sit on a beach and watch the waves lap against the shore. Sometimes marveling at the beauty of God's creation brings rejuvenation and joy. Try inviting Jesus along on a favorite pastime, such as fishing by a lake or watching a slow fire. Ask Jesus to teach you how to experience a time of calm in your day.

But do not be surprised if a host of reasons comes up to deter you from putting plans into action. Write down your thoughts or verbally tell Jesus what is on your mind. Then ask him to take care of these things until you return to your day. Ask Jesus to help you prioritize spending quality time with him. Ask him to help you see that you do not have to shoulder the troubles you face alone, that you can trust him to help you resolve the complications you face.

These are just a few suggestions on how you can rest in the love of Jesus. If none of these options appeals to you, or if these activities do not seem plausible, ask Jesus to direct you to possible places where you can dedicate a period of time to be with him so "that Christ may dwell in your [heart] through faith, as you are being rooted and grounded in love" (Ephesians 3:17).

2. Surrender through prayer. *Sometimes there comes a point when you just have to stop and take stock of your predicament. There comes a time when you don't know what to do and you are weary of being tired, overstressed, and overcommitted. It is in this moment of realization that you can experience the greatest freedom because you have acknowledged your need for assistance. This is the open door Jesus has been waiting for. He is ready to come in and help.*

Surrendering concerns to Jesus can take different forms. For some of us, writing our worries on a piece of paper and placing it at the foot of a cross offers relief. Others tell Jesus about their problems as if they are talking to a trusted confidant. This kind of conversation reminds them that they are not alone and that someone is indeed listening and supporting them through their trials. The form is not important. What is critical is that you are honest with Jesus. He wants you to come to him, just as you are.

When you give your concerns to Jesus, the challenge then is to wait, listen, and consider Jesus' words before planning and responding to the

situation. If Jesus can calm a storm, he can still the worries in your life. If he can walk on water, he can teach you to walk a life of faith. If he can feed five thousand people with two loaves of bread and a few fish, he can provide for you abundantly. When you surrender to Jesus' leadership, when you believe in the power of his name, his provision and wisdom and love will be more than enough.

"Very truly, I tell you, if you ask anything of the Father in my name, he will give it to you. Until now you have not asked for anything in my name. Ask and you will receive, so that your joy may be complete" (John 16:23b-24).

3. Be prepared to make changes. *You may well have to change something in your life if you want to reduce the stress in your life.*

When the pressures of life become your daily companion, when schedules dominate every waking moment, you may become so used to this rhythm of living that the idea of finding new ways of interacting with people and your troubles may seem daunting.

You may well find that you need to let go of some activities. This may entail cutting back on the way you spend money and use resources. You may decide to take a job that does not pay as well but gives you more time to spend with family and friends. You may exchange your car for a newer model less often, or live closer to your place of work to cut down on commuting time. Ask Jesus what new directions he would have you take to simplify your life.

Being under a lot of stress can lead to you make impulsive decisions that have far-reaching consequences. Let your emotions cool down before you deal with the matter at hand. This may require you to take a walk or take part in an activity that calms you. Ask Jesus to subdue your nervous energy and help you take into consideration the essential facts you need to consider before making an informed decision. Then prayerfully consider the following questions:

- Would this decision relieve my stress or intensify it?
- How might this decision influence my present and future plans?
- Can I financially afford this decision or would I be putting myself at financial risk that would add greater stress to my life?

- Would this decision be beneficial to my overall spiritual, emotional, and physical health, or would I be overextending myself?
- How would my decision affect those around me? Would it strengthen or weaken my relationships?
- Do I have at least two alternative plans if this situation does not work out the way I would like?

Ask Jesus to reveal the options that are available to you as you attempt to deal with the matter at hand. Don't let the pressures of life rush you into making hasty decisions. Take charge by relying on Jesus' wisdom to get you through those challenging, and sometimes unexpected, trials that can come your way.

Therefore, since we are surrounded by so great a cloud of witnesses, let us also lay aside every weight and the sin that clings so closely, and let us run with perseverance the race that is set before us, looking to Jesus the pioneer and perfecter of our faith. (Hebrews 12:1-2a)

4. Remember to praise God through it all. *Surrendering your stressful life to Jesus can come in the form of praise.*

In the face of stress, attempts to praise God may feel somewhat awkward. Your heart might be laden with sadness, making it difficult to feel like offering praise. Don't be discouraged. It is natural to feel this way, but I encourage you to keep on praising God, even when it does not make sense. In time, you will experience peace, even if your circumstances do not immediately change. In time, you will discover that Jesus is bigger than your problems, and he will get you through what you are dealing with. Ultimately, your praises can shift you into a restful state of mind, providing you with a sense of well-being and hope.

Praise activates your awareness that you are not alone. Praise ushers in thankfulness for God's promise to uphold you in his right hand (Psalm 63:8). Praise stimulates your understanding that God's love will help you not succumb to the stresses of your life: "You show me the path of life. In your presence there is fullness of joy; in your right hand are pleasures

forevermore" (Psalm 16:11). Praise harnesses your stress and inspires you to proclaim that "The LORD is my shepherd, I shall not want. He makes me lie down in green pastures; he leads me beside still waters; he restores my soul. He leads me in right paths for his name's sake" (Psalm 23:1-3).

You can sing praise songs to God (Psalm 147). You can lift your hands in adoration because "The LORD is gracious and merciful, slow to anger and abounding in steadfast love. The LORD is good to all, and his compassion is over all that he has made" (Psalm 145:8-9). You can dance or you can unleash your praise through loud words of adoration (Psalm 149). You may lie down or kneel and read scripture aloud, or treasure these words in your heart. You can be still and receive God's wisdom that invites you to "be still and know that [he is] God" (Psalm 46:10a). Playing music that proclaims Jesus' faithfulness and goodness can also uplift your soul (Psalm 150).

Whatever form of praise you adopt, your willingness to cultivate a life-style of praise will remind you that Jesus' power can give you the strength, vision, and wisdom to transcend the troubling events encircling your life. Receive peace in your praise and permit Jesus to comfort you with his words: "All things can be done for the one who believes" (Mark 9:23b).

5. Learn to say no to others and yes to Jesus. *If you want to de-stress your life, sometimes you will need to say no to people who want you to participate in a project or are in need of your assistance. Saying yes to Jesus means making him a priority. Seek his wisdom about your level of activity.*

Take an honest look at your schedule and consider carefully cutting back on those programs or activities that are contributing the greatest stress to your life. This may mean that you will have to make the difficult decision not to complete a task or fulfill a commitment. It is humbling to say "no" or "I can't" or "I don't know what to do," but you can ask Jesus to give you the courage to admit to others, to Jesus—and to yourself—what you can and cannot do. Utterances like these can draw you more intimately into the love of Jesus, whose compassion, grace, and forgiveness will assure you that he understands what you are going through and that he will help you make better choices in the future.

You may need to examine the reasons why you are so busy. Do you seek the approval of others? Do you associate your worth with what you do for a living or what you own? Do you fear disapproval or disappointing others? Do you think Jesus will love you more if you are constantly serving him by helping others? Learning to say no and learning to adopt wise choices about how you spend your time is a process, but Jesus can help you discover why you sometimes overcommit yourself. As you enter into a season of introspection, you will better understand why you make particular choices. This discovery will enable you to make informed decisions in the future about how you use your time, resources, and energy.

It is also useful to ask Jesus to help you respond to those who may not understand the choices you make. They may be disappointed or even express frustration or anger about your decisions. Ask Jesus to help you respond to them, and ask him to help you not judge yourself based on the opinions of others. The more you depend on Jesus' wisdom when deciding what projects you become involved with, the less you will be defined by the demands of your everyday life. Hold on to Jesus' promise: "Come to me, all you that are weary and are carrying heavy burdens, and I will give you rest" (Matthew 11:28).

6. Eat healthy food and exercise. *We don't often think of healthy eating and exercise as a spiritual priority. Yet scripture tells us, "Do you not know that your body is a temple of the Holy Spirit within you, which you have from God, and that you are not your own? For you were bought with a price; therefore glorify God in your body"(1 Corinthians 6:19).*

Are you getting enough sleep? What have you eaten in the last twenty-four hours? How much exercise have you been able to do this week? Your body is designed to be active; proper diet and exercise can energize you and instill in you a sense of well-being.

If this is an area of concern or neglect for you, remember how many times Jesus went away to rest. Remember that he took care to see that his followers were fed.

One note about this: Before changing your diet or launching into an exercise regime, check with a licensed physician or health professional

and gain their assistance in making appropriate adjustments to your way of life. When you visit these medical professionals, ask Jesus to accompany you and give you wisdom on how to make lifestyle changes that will honor him.

7. Enjoy social time with friends or family. *As with food and exercise, we may not think of "socializing" as a spiritual concern. Yet we are created for companionship and community.*

Jesus always made time for fellowship. Whether eating with his friends, his disciples, or someone he met for the first time, Jesus welcomed such interactions—even when they interrupted something he was doing. Follow the way of Jesus: He did not distance himself from people but rather sought them out. If you are someone who finds it difficult to socialize with others, share these concerns with Jesus. Ask Jesus to lead you to those whose company you can enjoy. Aim to live a life like the first Christians, whose practice of spending time with one another is documented in the book of Acts: "Day by day, as they spent much time together in the temple, they broke bread at home and ate their food with glad and generous hearts, praising God and having the goodwill of all the people. And day by day the lord added to their number those who were being saved" (Acts 2:46-47).

My prayer for you: I pray you will learn to trust Jesus with every aspect of your life. I pray your joy will be complete in him and that you will allow Jesus to help you lead a life that is less governed by stress and more infused with contentment and a quiet peace, knowing you are loved and cared for by a compassionate God. Amen.

2. ILLNESS

My stepfather, Dudley "Dougie" Byles, spent most of his adult life being employed in miserable jobs requiring back-breaking toil. But he never complained because he would do anything to secure the emotional and economic well-being of his family. He was a wonderful father, husband, brother, and friend. When he learned of his lung cancer, he prayed. We all prayed. For the most part, the doctors gave us little hope, yet we cried out to Jesus and found comfort in the knowledge that Jesus was with us.

In the early stages of his diagnosis, Dougie continued to supervise the "DIY" jobs that needed to be completed. He got up every morning and fed the dogs. He cooked. He liked to garden. He socialized with his friends. He attended Sunday church services. He and my mother watched their favorite daytime soaps. They laughed together, shared stories, and played dominoes. Such was Dougie's hopeful outlook on life that one could almost forget he was ill.

Apart from the occasional times when his breathing was a little labored, Dougie had been doing fine until his third exposure to chemotherapy. The potency of the drugs traveling through his body sapped him of energy and opened him to a level of pain that he had never endured before. At that point he began to lose his ability to do the things that he enjoyed, and the slow breakdown of his health started to ravage his body. During those bleak days of discouragement, when the medication did not ease his suffering, Dougie struggled to see the brighter side of his condition. The reality of his illness, the aggressive nature of his cancer meant that no matter how hard he tried, he could not deny his agony or sadness about this fateful turn of events in his life.

Through all the hardship, what impressed me most about Dougie was that, until the last moments of his life, he never lost his desire to live. He continued to enjoy the harvest of his garden. Dougie often said he was thankful that God had allowed him to see and eat from every tree

and plant that he had nurtured from infancy. Dougie also found ways to engage with the people he loved and to marvel at the world around him. Participating in social gatherings was still important to him. Until the last couple of months of his life, he mustered up enough strength to go to church every Sunday. For all his intention to live life to the fullest, he exercised wisdom when he realized that he was not as strong as he used to be. He accepted the very real way his illness weakened him and did not take risks with his health. When he became tired, he rested. When he could no longer maintain his garden or take care of his dogs, he hired someone to help him carry out these tasks. And yet, regardless of these setbacks, he continued to appreciate the beauty of his surroundings.

It brought Dougie great joy to know that people from around the world were praying for him. Such news rejuvenated him and shored up his faith. Throughout his illness, Dougie knew Jesus was his strength. He knew Jesus loved him. He believed that when it was his time to go home, he would be spending eternity in heaven. This knowledge gave Dougie such peace that he was able to buoy the spirit of others. He made people laugh. He shared words of encouragement with friends, family, and acquaintances. His faith in Jesus inspired others to live life with purpose and joy. Even as he fought for his very breath, his love for life breathed a new awareness in people to treat each day as a gift. After spending time with Dougie, you could not help but come away with the thought that the greatest gift of all could be found in Jesus' love.

All the while, my mother cared for her beloved husband. Apart from a few occasions when she could not get to the hospital, they rarely missed reading the Bible together and praying every morning. Their love for Jesus formed a core part of their marriage, and day by day, moment by moment, they were aware of the importance of looking to Jesus to shepherd them throughout the good and trying times. They needed Jesus before this illness, and they needed Jesus even more during this trial.

As my mother nursed Dougie, sorrow came to the surface. Yet, like Dougie, my mother never stopped praying. She asked Jesus to heal her husband, but throughout the course of his illness, she also prayed about her fear of being alone. In the last days of Dougie's life, she began a prayer of surrender, asking that Jesus' will be done.

One night she asked me to join her in praying that Jesus would bring someone to help her care for Dougie. That night Jesus came, and Dougie died. As my mother stroked his hand, peace cast a veil over his face. His final breath was not halting, but a long, deep sigh that testified he was now at rest.

Between the death and the funeral, I asked Jesus why he had not answered our prayers to spare Dougie's life. There were times when I did not feel the presence of Jesus. Yet, eventually, I had a sense of Jesus loving me and comforting me through my grief.

Looking back, I know that Jesus' love supported us as a family. Jesus gave Dougie the stamina to live two years longer than medical professionals had predicted. And in those two years, I told Dougie many times how much I loved and appreciated him as my surrogate father. Jesus also gave my mother time to come to terms with the possibility that her beloved husband might not be healed of his cancer and she would lose him to death. After two years of talking with him and caring for him, after two years of enjoying his company and crying with him, she was more ready than she would have been if he had died two years earlier.

It is often in the quiet moments of my day that I find myself being even more grateful that Jesus gave Dougie the desires of his heart: he lived and died in the homeland he loved. Dougie drew his last breath in the home he and my mother had local craftsmen build. He died with his loving wife by his side, and with dignity. Best of all, Dougie died knowing that Jesus loved him.

I cannot anticipate how Jesus will comfort you when you deal with illness in your life or in your family. I do not know how Jesus will minister to you as you cope with the daily reality of a friend, relative, acquaintance, colleague, or loved one who is suffering from a terminal sickness, nor how you will react in grief. You may not feel Jesus' presence when you call out to him. You may live through seasons where the question "Why?" punctuates your waking moments. You may come into contact with people who say inappropriate things or who are insensitive to your struggles. What I do know is that, through it all, Jesus is more than willing to hear whatever is on your heart. He can handle your questions, carry your distress, take on your pain, and enter into your disappointments, anger, doubts, and fears.

You are not alone. Jesus' love can and will be your resting place and anchor. When you schedule doctor appointments, confer with specialists, seek the opinions of consultants, take medication, undergo aggressive treatments, receive physical therapy, recuperate, sift through the news of medical breakthroughs, receive counseling, grapple with medical bills, fill out insurance forms, convalesce, or adapt to a new diet, know that every step of the way, Jesus is with you. He can bring friends, relatives, health care workers, medical professionals, bystanders, members of the church, even perfect strangers to support and walk alongside you in your time of need. Be encouraged. Jesus will be your mainstay, your joy, comfort, and hope. Keep on praying and let Jesus know your needs. For Jesus' love is enough to get you through this season.

In scripture we are told of many healings at the hands of Jesus.
Give yourself a few minutes to picture this scene
of Jesus responding to the faith of an unnamed woman:

"If I but touch his clothes, I will be made well."(Mark 5:28)

The tightly packed throng can feel each other's breath against their skin. Shoulder to shoulder, arm to arm, they push their way to Jesus. The weight of their demands, the force of their need, and the sheer mass of their presence almost crushes him. Still, not an utterance of complaint comes out of his mouth.

Facing this tide of bodies, a woman steps into the current of the crowd. For twelve years she has worn the name of unnoticed and borne the label of an outcast. She reaches out behind Jesus. Her fingertips brush against his garment like a whisper. At once, the bleeding that has marked her existence for twelve years stops flowing. Aware of her healing, she feels as if the midday sun has decided to shine at dawn.

Her presence does not go unnoticed, for Jesus desires to see the one whose fingerprints are embroidered onto his cloak. Into the marrow of the crowd, Jesus inserts the question, "Who touched my clothes?" (Mark 5:30b). The disciples wonder how he can feel the touch of a single person in that crowd, yet Jesus continues his search.

Drawn by the concern in his voice, the woman journeys out of the coarse tapestry of the crowd. Scared and shaking, unsure of Jesus' reaction, the woman falls at his feet and tells him "the whole truth" (Mark 5:33b) and he listens. Her fears vanish and peace enfolds her as he proclaims her healed. And when he publicly honors this formerly invisible person for her faith, it is as if he adorns her with a robe woven with peace, bearing her proper name: Beloved Daughter of Faith.

CHOOSE HOPE

And a large crowd followed him and pressed in on him. Now there was a woman who had been suffering from hemorrhages for twelve years. She had endured much under many physicians, and had spent all that she had; and she was no better, but rather grew worse. (Mark 5:24b-26)

The woman described in this Mark passage must have been a woman of considerable wealth and resourcefulness——after all, she had sought the advice of "many physicians." She had been able to take advantage of all that the medical profession had to offer for twelve years. Yet all the methods, diagnoses, and treatments had not healed her. By the time she met Jesus, she had "spent all that she had." Quite possibly, her desperation to be healed had left her penniless and without possessions, and still she suffered hemorrages.

The woman probably lived in a constant state of worry, embarrassment, and shame. The pungent smell emanating from her blood doubtless clung to her body and clothes, and the lingering odor must have only added to the stigma. Because she was unable to stop the steady discharge of blood, many people likely considered her tainted and, therefore, untouchable. She might even have been treated as diseased as a leper. For twelve long years, she had endured this ostracism, suffering both emotional and physical pain.

It is not hard to imagine that this woman felt like a failure. Maybe her years as an outcast had made her reluctant to be with other people. Family members, community residents, childhood friends may well have distanced themselves from her. But somehow she knew she could stand close to Jesus. She was willing to risk the ridicule and rejection of those around her to get to him. In that decision she chose to find hope.

Have there been times when you have been concerned about what people might think of you if you sought Jesus' help? Or you may have kept close friends and family at a distance as you tried to cope with your illness. Maybe you find it difficult to admit your weaknesses to others. You may be reluctant to admit that your ideas and efforts have not worked. Whatever your plight, whatever you are dealing with, it is not too much

for Jesus. He will not cringe from you, or criticize you, or reject you. As with the unnamed woman, Jesus is there for you. You can come to him without fear. You, too, can make the decision to choose hope.

PRAYER

Jesus, thank you that no matter the condition I find myself in, you always want to touch me, love me, and serve me. Thank you that you want to draw close to me. Your words assure me that you are more than able to turn around my circumstances. Amen.

"IF . . ."

She had heard about Jesus, and came up behind him in the crowd and touched his cloak, for she said, "If I but touch his clothes, I will be made well." (Mark 5:27-28)

What had this woman heard about Jesus? Did someone tell her that Jesus healed anyone who came to him? Did a bystander reveal to her that Jesus touched the untouchables? Did someone share with her that Jesus was compassionate? Whatever she had heard, her determination to be near Jesus speaks volumes.

She was certain that "if" she just brushed the exterior of Jesus' garments, she would be made well. There was no doubt in her mind about Jesus' ability to transform her life. At the same time, she placed no demands on *how* Jesus should heal her. Neither did she state *when* she expected her illness to depart from her body. Her expectation of how and when Jesus would bring healing to her body was as unconditional as her willingness to yield to his power.

With conviction she declared, "If I but touch his clothes, I will be made well." Even *before* touching his outer garment, she knew in the deepest recesses of her heart that she would fully recover from her illness. The "if" in her statement had more to do with her courage to reach out to be relieved of her suffering than with her belief in Jesus. Even though she had traveled to be near him, she still had to take the final step to be healed by him. She still had to stretch out her hands and touch his clothing. Did she have the courage to take that life-changing step and stand in Jesus' presence?

If. This word invites us to consider whether we are ready to trust Jesus to bring healing into our lives. Think about the woman's touch. There was no spoken request, no stipulation as to what areas of her life she wanted Jesus to heal. She just wanted to be made well. When we come to Jesus for healing, we are giving Jesus room to touch those parts of our lives that we might not even know are in need of healing.

What are your "ifs"? Maybe you struggle with doubt. Maybe you have asked Jesus for healing and did not see immediate benefits. Maybe you

fear that he might not come through for you. Whatever prevents you from seeking Jesus' healing touch, ask Jesus for courage, for trust, so you can be open to the healing you need.

PRAYER

Jesus, help me trust your ability to heal every part of my life. Give me the courage to reach out and receive your care for me. Amen.

AN INTIMATE CONNECTION

Immediately her hemorrhage stopped; and she felt in her body that she was healed of her disease. (Mark 5:29)

This courageous woman managed to push her way through the throng and find a place near Jesus. Bolstered by faith and hope, she stepped forward and gingerly reached out to feel the hem of his coat. She probably did not look around to see if anybody was looking. Her touch surely went unnoticed by the crowd.

The results were immediate: Her hemorrhaging ceased to flow through her body. No one had to tell her she was healed; her body became the voice of affirmation. We can only imagine the emotional release she experienced. Elation, relief, and joy must have coursed through her when the weight of twelve years of illness lifted.

Those who have struggled with an illness often testify that they have become more aware of their bodies and how their bodies work. Yet we may not be as sensitive to the ways in which Jesus can bring healing to our minds and souls. When we reach out to Jesus, the changes may not appear immediately. But in time we will discover that his love has transformed us.

Just as the woman's healing began with a touch, it is through an intimate connection with Jesus, spending time with him, reading scripture, pondering his teaching, participating in a conversation with him through prayer, that he can teach you how to live in his healing. Initiate the conversation with a time of gratitude. Ask Jesus to remind you how he has brought healing to your life. Thank him for all he has done and will continue to do in your life.

PRAYER

Jesus, I am grateful that you respond immediately to my touch. Help me to be grateful for what you have done and to wait in anticipation of what you will do in the future. Amen.

"HERE I AM"

Immediately aware that power had gone forth from him, Jesus turned about in the crowd and said, "Who touched my clothes?" And his disciples said to him, "You see the crowd pressing in on you; how can you say, 'Who touched me?'" (Mark 5:30-31)

"Who touched me?" Jesus wanted to discover the identity of the person who touched him, but the disciples thought it was an impossible task. After all, there was an entire multitude vying for Jesus' attention. Yet nothing or no one could prevent Jesus from feeling the presence of his people.

Only Jesus can be in the midst of a crowd and still be attentive to each individual. Only Jesus observes and understands fully the multi-faceted character of every person. So when you hear the words "Who touched me?" know that Jesus is asking because he wants to know you in a deeper way. Jesus is always aware of your existence; you are important to him. No matter how many people are trying to get his attention, he will always be aware of your cares and wants. Your answer can be as simple as "here I am." In response, Jesus will stand by your side, hear your concerns, and bring hope into your life.

If you are struggling with illness and wonder how much it matters to Jesus, be assured that Jesus senses your presence. You are not "lost in the crowd." He feels you reaching out to touch him, and he wants to know you. He will always have enough time for you and will call out to you to come to him.

PRAYER

Jesus, help me to cry out to you when I need help. Thank you for being exquisitely attentive to my presence. Amen.

THE WHOLE TRUTH

He looked all around to see who had done it. But the woman, knowing what had happened to her, came in fear and trembling, fell down before him, and told him the whole truth. (Mark 5:32-33)

Whatever the woman's thoughts, whatever her apprehensions, one thing is evident: She did not doubt for a second that she had been cured of her disease. One would think that after enduring twelve years of illness, she would have shouted for joy, letting everyone know that she had been healed. And yet she kept silent. Perhaps after spending so many years of trying not to draw attention to herself, of experiencing ridicule and judgment, she had forgotten what it was like to share her trials and triumphs.

So when Jesus called her out of the crowd, she came forward with "fear and trembling." Yet once in his presence, she fell down before him and told him "the whole truth." In the midst of the crowd, this woman bared her soul to the One who had restored her health.

We do not know what she told Jesus; we only know that she told him the whole truth. And in response, Jesus pondered her words with the same kind of attention that he paid to discovering her identity in the crowd. This is how Jesus desires to interact with you. He wants to know you, the whole truth about you.

If you are dealing with a physical illness, take comfort in the knowledge that Jesus wants to hear everything about your life. You may feel that you are burdening him with your concerns. Or you may be so focused on your disability that it does not occur to you to share with Jesus other aspects of your life. Or you might feel so unworthy or so downhearted that you avoid coming to him.

Alternately, if you are taking care of someone who is ill, you may feel you are allowed to pray only about that person's struggles and not your own. You may even feel selfish or ashamed of your own needs.

Take special note of this passage: Jesus made no stipulations about what the woman *ought* to tell him. He did not probe her with questions;

he simply invited her company. This is Jesus' invitation to you as well. You can share with him your desires, wants, temptations, frustrations, anger, and concerns. There is not one area of your life that Jesus does not want to minister to, touch, or heal. His attentiveness will remind you that you are more than your illness.

PRAYER

Jesus, thank you that I can tell you everything about my life. Amen.

CHILD OF GOD

He said to her, "Daughter, your faith has made you well; go in peace, and be healed of your disease." (Mark 5:34)

After the woman had communicated her truth, Jesus responded by calling her "Daughter." Even though this was Jesus' first encounter with the woman, this one word conveyed that he treasured her as a member of his own family, and that he identified her as God's daughter. Until this moment, countless people had treated her as less than a second-class citizen. Jesus' love rescued her from this shame. The stigma, the gossip, the shroud of contempt following her every move were of no concern to Jesus. He did not hesitate to interact with this woman whom many considered damaged and untouchable.

Jesus also affirmed her by telling her in front of a crowd of people that it was her faith that "made [her] well." This, in effect, was a public announcement that her illness did not define her. She was a woman of faith *before* she received physical healing. He then told her to go in peace, assuring her that she could move on with her life, that she was no longer held hostage by her disease. It was by Jesus' authority that she finally received the fullness of healing.

Illness has a tendency to take over everything else in life. Doctors' offices, hospitals, tests, and therapies all have a way of overshadowing the days—especially if your illness stretches over a period of time. Take heart from this woman's story. Jesus does not identify you by your illness but calls you a daughter or son. Hold fast to the assurance that you are valued. Let the love of Jesus fill the parts of you that feel unloved and unlovely. Breathe in his peace.

PRAYER

Jesus, what a comfort it is to know that you want to honor me. Thank you that you will never be ashamed of me. Teach me how to claim and live in the identity that I am a child of God, both in the present and future. Amen.

YOUR POINT OF NEED

One of the leaders of the synagogue named Jairus came and, when he saw him, fell at his feet and begged him repeatedly, "My little daughter is at the point of death. Come and lay your hands on her, so that she may be made well, and live." So he went with him. (Mark 5:21-24)

As a leader of the local synagogue, Jairus must have had access to some of the best minds around. And yet he threw himself onto the ground at Jesus' feet, sullying his fine garments and imploring Jesus to heal his dying daughter. Jairus was not too proud to publicly declare his faith in Jesus' powers to heal. His display of emotion was unabashed, raw, and unapologetic. His daughter was dying, and he was desperate.

If not for this family tragedy, Jairus might never have sought the presence of Jesus. Yet Jesus did not stop to judge. Without hesitation, he followed Jairus to the house where his daughter lay.

Regardless of social status, age, or ethnic origin, Jesus turned no one away. Jesus will not turn you away either. Jesus is willing to hear and respond to your cries. Jesus has enough time for you. No obstacle is too big. It does not matter what you look like. It does not matter what you do for a living or what emotional state you are in. All that matters is that Jesus' love is enough.

Perhaps, like Jairus, you have a child who is seriously ill, or you know a friend or a family member who is battling a terminal disease. You may feel helpless and at a loss about what you can do. Or you may be wrestling with an illness yourself. Whatever your ordeal, you can ask Jesus to come to the place where you need him most. Jesus will follow you and meet you at your point of need. Do not let any thought or complication get in the way of telling Jesus precisely what you want from him.

PRAYER

Jesus, thank you that no matter what I am going through, you are always willing to help me. Give me the unabashed heart of Jairus to call on you, and keep reminding me that you will always come to my aid. Amen.

"ONLY BELIEVE"

While he was still speaking, some people came from the leader's house to say, "Your daughter is dead. Why trouble the teacher any further?" But overhearing what they said, Jesus said to the leader of the synagogue, "Do not fear, only believe." (Mark 5:35-36)

Here's the scenario: Jairus begged Jesus to come to his house to heal his beloved child and Jesus agreed to go with him. But on the way to Jairus's house, Jesus stopped to heal the woman who touched him in the crowd. What was Jairus thinking when Jesus focused on another follower in need? Whatever his opinions, Jairus did not interrupt Jesus or impress upon him the urgency of getting to his daughter.

But it seemed that the delay in getting to Jairus's house had tragic consequences. While Jesus was still speaking to the woman, messengers informed Jairus that his daughter had passed away, and they advised him not to trouble the teacher any longer. Jesus overheard what was being said and consoled Jairus, saying, "Do not fear, only believe."

Have you ever been in a situation where it seemed Jesus paid more attention to the needs of others than your own? Have you wondered whether Jesus heard your pleas for help? Perhaps you have been angry with Jesus when it seemed he turned a deaf ear to your cries. Take heart. This passage reveals that Jesus never forgets or dismisses any of our concerns.

Notice that Jesus first acknowledged Jairus's struggle with fear before calling upon his faith: "Do not fear, only believe." Jesus understands what you are going through. Tell Jesus about the feelings of fear and anxiety you are battling. Ask him to help you believe that he is never too busy to hear your cry and respond to your concerns. Ask him to turn your fears into hope. Ask him to help you believe and experience in a tangible way that his "perfect love casts out fear" (1 John 4:18).

Remember, Jesus loves you and will never desert you.

PRAYER

Jesus, thank you for wanting to free me from the grip of fear. Teach me to believe in you when I am going through difficult trials. Meet me at my place of need and help me trust you, even in the midst of my doubts. Amen.

THE POWER OF HOPE

He allowed no one to follow him except Peter, James, and John, the brother of James. When they came to the house of the leader of the synagogue, he saw a commotion, people weeping and wailing loudly. When he had entered, he said to them, "Why do you make a commotion and weep? The child is not dead but sleeping." And they laughed at him. (Mark 5:37-40a)

As Jesus approached the house where Jairus's daughter had just died, people were weeping. Jesus acknowledged their heart-wrenching cries by asking, "Why do you make a commotion and weep? The child is not dead but sleeping." Jesus' words were met with laughter, for the people considered his declaration unbelievable, even ridiculous. Yet Jesus did not take offense. His single focus was on healing this child; he dismissed everyone except the child's father, mother, and the three disciples with him.

When you face illness or grief—your own or someone else's—it is natural to feel sad. You may feel dismayed when you receive difficult news about someone battling an illness. You may feel like giving up if you hear a particularly disheartening prognosis. Your faith may flounder, and Jesus' promises about caring for you may seem ridiculous. Or, if you insist on believing in Jesus' healing powers, some people may mock your beliefs.

This is precisely the time to turn to Jesus. Tell him what you are feeling and ask him to show you how he is present to your circumstances. Ask him to instill hope in you. Ask him for comfort and the ability to trust what he can do. This does not mean denying your circumstances. Rather, it means believing that Jesus will fortify your faith, enabling you to hold onto a hope that rises above the adversity you endure.

And, just as Jesus invited Peter, John, and James to accompany him on portions of his faith journey, so follow his lead and surround yourself with people who can support your Christian convictions.

PRAYER

Jesus, help me to trust you even when my prognosis seems dire. Show me how I can hope in you as I confront my illness. Amen.

THE MIRACLE OF LOVE

He took her by the hand and said to her, "Talitha cum," which means, "Little girl, get up!" And immediately the girl got up and began to walk about (she was twelve years of age). At this they were overcome with amazement. He strictly ordered them that no one should know this, and told them to give her something to eat. (Mark 5:41-43)

Even though this child was caught in the grip of death, Jesus placed her hand into his and uttered the instructions, "Little girl, get up!" And the twelve-year-old girl stepped out of her bed and walked about the room. Her father, mother, and the disciples must have watched in amazement as they witnessed this child freed from death. We can only imagine how they reacted. Her parents may have embraced the girl, swinging her around in delight. She may have stretched her arms in the air and skipped around the room. She may have hugged each person who witnessed her healing. The disciples may have been stunned into silence—or responded with cheers.

Jesus' response to this miracle was humility. His only instruction to those gathered was that they not tell anyone what they had just witnessed. Rather than draw attention to himself, Jesus was concerned with the overall welfare of the child; he instructed her parents to get her something to eat.

Just as Jesus recognized that the little girl needed food, so he will anticipate your needs before you do. If you are coping with illness, ask Jesus to help you be aware of how he is attentive to the details of your everyday comings and goings. Ask him to help you appreciate that all aspects of your life are touched by the miracle of his love and care. Ask him to feed you spiritually and emotionally with his love. For Jesus' love is the food of life that will maintain you in and through all that you confront.

PRAYER

Jesus, feed me with your love and fill me with your hope. Thank you for being a God of details. Amen.

COMFORTING WORDS

One day, while he was teaching, Pharisees and teachers of the law were sitting near by (they had come from every village of Galilee and Judea and from Jerusalem); and the power of the LORD was with him to heal. (Luke 5:17)

The Apostle Luke tells us that the Pharisees and teachers of the law journeyed from far and wide to hear Jesus' teachings. Yet it is curious that Luke specifies that they sat "near by." Maybe they could not push their way through the massive crowds. Or perhaps they did not have a compelling desire to draw close to Jesus. Unlike many who traveled to see Jesus, they might not have considered themselves in need of his healing.

Yet they came. Did they want to hear what he had to say, to ponder his words in their hearts? Did they ever understand his healing power? Or did they want to use his teachings to discredit and entrap him?

Like these Pharisees and teachers of the law, we, too, may seek out Jesus' wisdom yet fail to experience the healing power of his words. We may have a Bible on the shelf, but if we never read it, we will miss the stories of healing and forgiveness permeating Jesus' ministry. We won't experience Jesus' calming presence, tender voice, and healing touch. It would be like being in a room with someone who is talking, but because we are so preoccupied with our own thoughts, we never hear what they are saying.

Sometimes the worry or pain of illness can lock you in a room of spiritual despondency or indifference. If you find yourself in that place, consider asking a friend or a family member to partner with you in reading scripture. Or read just a few verses at a time. Ask Jesus to point you to those passages that can nurture you and instill hope. Ask Jesus to deepen your awareness of his healing presence so you can live more fully in the comfort of his word.

PRAYER

Jesus, help me be open to your teaching. With your wisdom, guide me to what you want me to hear from you. Thank you for the comfort I can find in your words. Amen.

PRAYER IN MOTION

Just then some men came, carrying a paralyzed man on a bed. They were trying to bring him in and lay him before Jesus. (Luke 5:18)

The men who carried the paralyzed man had a single focus: getting him to Jesus. Set in their resolve, they worked together as a team. The Apostle Luke does not reveal whether these men were friends nor how long they had known the man they carried. Nor do we know how long or how far they had traveled. We only know that these men were willing to carry this man who would have been seen by many as broken, weak, damaged, and untouchable. In their own strength, they could not have met the physical and spiritual needs of this man, but together they could go to Jesus.

The carriers' determination symbolizes the power of intercessory prayer. They exercise a proactive rather than a passive faith. Their actions of cradling this man's body between them evoke an image of God's love. Their servanthood embodies hands-on prayer in motion.

If you are battling an illness, or have experienced illness in the past, you know how valuable it is for others to intercede on your behalf. When others partner with you to present your needs to Jesus, their faith can invigorate yours. Their prayers can lift your spirits. And their willingness to serve—by running errands and meeting practical needs—is prayer in motion.

Whatever your feelings about the issues surrounding your condition, or whatever obstacles you face, ask Jesus to lead you to others who can pray for you and lift your concerns to him. Ask Jesus to send people who will help you in your time of need. Trust that you are not alone, because Jesus and his servants are with you.

PRAYER

Jesus, teach me how to stay focused on you. Help me to keep bringing my troubles and needs to you. Thank you for the people who pray on my behalf—both in words and deeds. Amen.

ON THE RECEIVING END

*Finding no way to bring him in because of the crowd, they went up on the roof
and let him down with his bed through the tiles into the middle of the crowd in
front of Jesus. (Luke 5:19)*

This was one determined group. While still carrying the paralyzed man,
these men climbed up a wall to the roof, then lowered the mattress down
until the man rested on the ground before the feet of Jesus. No words of
complaint from the man on the bed. No frustrated mutterings from the
carriers. Just a single-minded persistence—and belief in the One they
were trying to reach. The carriers did not rely on their own powers to
find a solution to this man's physical ailments; they were united in the
belief that only Jesus could help this man struck down by disability.

Just as the tiles on the roof made the carriers' attempts to get the
paralyzed man to Jesus more difficult, sometimes we, too, may have
to confront and go through obstacles before we can finally meet with
Jesus. We may need to rely on the faith of others to get us there. We may
encounter strangers who help us reach the loving presence of Jesus. Like
the paralyzed man, we need to be able to *receive* this help.

When you are coping with an illness, you may feel crippled by a
sense of hopelessness. You may be afraid to undergo a particular form
of medical care or become weary of the battery of treatments you are
receiving. You might find the technical information related to your illness
overwhelming. How willing are you to acknowledge your need and invite
others to partner with you in your struggles? When others offer to help,
how willing are you to let yourself be carried? How willing are you to be
brought to Jesus?

Ask Jesus not only to bring people to you who will physically care for
you but also to open you to receiving their care. Let their acts of servanthood remind you that Jesus values you and wants to touch you when you
are hurting. As you take in their care, be assured that whatever you face,
you are not alone.

PRAYER

Jesus, thank you that you know what I need even before I cry out to you for assistance. Help me to be dependent on you for my healing, even as I welcome the partnership of others who are willing to look after me. And when I find it hard to receive the care of others, help me to see you in their acts of service. Amen.

TAKE HEART

When Jesus saw their faith, he said to the paralytic, "Take heart, son; your sins are forgiven." (Matthew 9:1b-2)

While Jesus recognized the faith of those who placed the paralytic man before him, he directed his words to the man lying on the mat. He could see the man was a paralytic, yet his first words did not address the man's physical condition but his spiritual well-being. Compassion underlined Jesus' words: "Take heart, son." By calling this man "son," Jesus expressed this man's immeasurable value. The title of son changed his status from that of a disabled man to God's child. His core identity was no longer defined by how ill he was but by how loved he was by God, for as far as Jesus was concerned, God always saw this man as his son, his child.

After uttering these words of mercy, Jesus made a powerful statement of freedom: "Your sins are forgiven." Jesus looked beyond the man's physical state and saw a deeper place in need of healing. He focused his attention on the heart and the soul of the man and saw his need for forgiveness. No matter who we are, no matter what our physical condition, we are all in need of that forgiveness.

If you are coping with an illness, be open to the particular ways Jesus will address your request for healing. As a son or daughter of God, you are of infinite worth. Jesus knows your heart and soul, and he knows the physical and emotional healing you need. Ask Jesus if there is an area of your life that you need to surrender to him. And as you do so, remember that your physical ailment has not emerged because Jesus wants to punish you for the past wrongs you may have committed. Your surrender to Jesus will enable you to draw closer to his love as you learn to trust and depend on him for your life and emotional, physical, and spiritual well-being. Then as a child of God, live in the freedom of knowing that Jesus forgives you.

PRAYER

Jesus, thank you that no matter what I am going through, you love me as your child. Thank you that you stand ready, always, to forgive my shortcomings and heal my heart. Amen.

DEALING WITH ILLNESS

The following guidelines offer some ideas for how to faithfully cope with your illness. Whatever strategies you decide to employ, I encourage you to pray and ask Jesus to pour out his wisdom and counsel you. As you live with illness, ask Jesus to shepherd you through this trying time and give you a sense of wholeness in spirit.

1. Pray for healing. Whether you are struck with illness, or someone you know is living with an ailment, pray for healing on all levels—spiritual, physical, and emotional.

Whatever illness you face, prayer can be the healing balm that gets you through the difficult seasons. If there are times when you wonder whether Jesus hears your prayers or is responding to your pleas for help, remember that Jesus has promised that he will always hear you and attend to your needs.

If you find yourself attached to a particular outcome in your prayers, ask Jesus for guidance on how to pray. Ask for sensitivity to know how Jesus might want to guide you through the circumstances you are confronting. Ask him to open you to new ways of seeing the important issues. Ask him to help you trust that his love and direction will uphold you no matter what you face.

And don't forget to ask others to partner with you in prayer. Confide in trusted individuals who love Jesus; they can provide you with additional discernment as you make decisions about your treatment and illness.

2. Partner with others. Allow Jesus to guide you to those who can help support you in seasons of illness.

Ask Jesus to shepherd you to the health professionals who will care for you. Before you visit the hospital or see a medical professional, pray that Jesus will pour out his wisdom upon these medical consultants and guide them as they treat you.

Also ask Jesus to bring people to you who can offer assistance. Maybe you need someone to drive you to and from the hospital, to pick up your medication from the pharmacy, to run daily errands such as grocery

shopping, or to clean your home. Maybe you need someone to help you fill out complicated medical forms. Maybe you need help with your correspondence with insurance companies. These tangible gifts of servanthood can offer you much-needed comfort and bring a measure of healing in your moments of need.

3. Socialize with others. *Conversation over a meal or a cup of tea or coffee, attending a support group for those who are coping with a similar illness, going for a walk or going to the movies with a friend are just some of the activities that can provide you with much-needed relief from the day-to-day challenges of dealing with illness.*

Despite the many demands on his ministry, Jesus never underestimated the importance of spending time with others. He understood the necessity for us to support one another and share one another's burdens.

If you feel caught up in the intensity of an illness, whether you or someone you love is sick, sharing even the most mundane events can renew your outlook on life. Let the understanding and counsel of those who have experienced similar circumstances assure you that you are not the first to encounter what you are going through. Let their laughter raise your spirit. Let hearing about their difficult times put your own challenges into a broader context. And always ask Jesus to join you in these activities.

> *"I give you a new commandment, that you love one another. Just as I have loved you, you also should love one another. By this everyone will know that you are my disciples, if you have love for one another." (John 13:34-35)*

4. Confide in others about your true feelings toward your struggles. *Remember, even Jesus wept. Don't be hard on yourself if you are feeling a sense of hopelessness.*

As you face the ramifications of your illness, give to Jesus any anger, confusion, or doubts you may be feeling—including your doubts about Jesus' ability to come to your aid. Jesus understands.

If you are feeling overwhelmed by your circumstances and want to give up on yourself and on life, it is important not to keep these sentiments

to yourself. Confiding in a counselor, reaching out to a pastor or a priest, or seeking help from trusted friends or relatives can provide you with the support you need. If you do not ask for help, you run the risk of being consumed by these thoughts and sinking into a state of despair.

You do not have to downplay your emotions; you can bring all that you are, and all that you feel, to Jesus. And he can help you take the steps you need to get the comfort and support you need.

5. Take time to rest. *Illness is debilitating on many levels. You may not think of rest as a spiritual priority, but even Jesus rested. Prioritizing times of rest is essential to nourish and maintain your sense of well-being.*

When you are dealing with an illness, any number of factors can rob you of energy. Your ailments can strip you of strength. If you have to undergo a number of treatments and are required to make frequent visits to see any number of specialists, while still juggling other responsibilities, you may feel physically drained. Emotionally, you can become discouraged or worry about how your loved ones are coping with your illness. You might become so concerned about the welfare of others that you feel you have to be strong for them and try not to show any signs of weakness.

Similarly, if you are the caregiver for someone who is ill, you may become emotionally and physically weary. Exhaustion can cause irritability. Fatigue can lead to a state of depression. You may feel guilty for wanting to take some time off from your loved one's struggles. You might not seek the support you need because you consider this a sign of failure.

But remember that even Jesus rested. When the demands of ministry were pressing, Jesus took time to go to a lonely place and spend time with God. Follow Jesus' example. Allow Jesus to lead you into a period where you can be comforted by him. You may need to learn to compromise by relying on others to take care of some things for you so you can rest. You may need to give yourself permission not to be everything to the person you are caring for. Ask Jesus to direct you to those who can help you carve out some time for the recuperation you need.

6. Read scripture. *Reflecting on scripture can give you food for thought and inspire you in and out of difficult seasons in your life.*

When you are feeling discouraged about your illness, ask Jesus to lead you to portions of scripture that will encourage you. Take solace in reading about how Jesus came to the aid of others. Ask Jesus what he would have you learn from the scriptures.

If you feel distant from what you are reading, try imagining yourself in the story; see yourself as a participant. This can make scripture more relevant to your experience. Then ask Jesus to teach you how to apply his teachings to your life.

Just as you require food, rest, and medical care, so you need scripture to nourish you.

> *"I will meditate on your precepts,*
> *and fix my eyes on your ways.*
> *I will delight in your statutes;*
> *I will not forget your word.*
> *Deal bountifully with your servant,*
> *so that I may live and observe your word."(Psalm 119:15-17)*

7. Praise God through your sickness. *This may be a difficult suggestion to embrace when you are in pain, especially if you feel abandoned by Jesus in the midst of your suffering.*

Even when you are feeling down-hearted or in pain, I encourage you to tell Jesus how you feel and ask him to help you praise God. Although it might feel impossible, awkward—or even dishonest—at first, praise can uplift your spirit. Praising God can lift you up from the mire of any emotion that threatens to take away your trust in Jesus' healing presence. Praise awakens your spiritual senses, despite the afflictions you are burdened with.

When you praise God, you honor Jesus. When you cherish Jesus, you revere God. As you seek to adore Jesus, your experience of his goodness will deepen. In time, you will see and feel and hear Jesus come to your assistance in ways that you never thought possible. A sense of well-being will grow as you experience a peace that may even baffle you at times. So

keep on praising God for, in time, the power of Jesus will heighten your awareness of what he can do in your life.

Part of coping with your illness may require you to explore alternate means of praise. If you are bedridden, you can still speak words of reverence to God. You can praise God in silence (Psalm 49:3) or recite scripture, such as "LORD, you have been our dwelling place in all generations. Before the mountains were brought forth, or ever you had formed the earth and the world, from everlasting to everlasting you are God" (Psalm 90:1-2). You might close your eyes and sing a hymn or a gospel song, either from memory or from a hymnal. Take heart; you may be immobile, but God is your dwelling place.

You might also ask someone to write in bold letters verses from scripture or lyrics of praise songs on banners, or placards and attach them to the ceiling and/or walls of the room where you spend most of your time. You could have someone read scripture to you, or you could listen to an audio recording of the Bible, or you might ask a friend to record some portions of scripture so these words are perpetually instilling hope in you (Psalm 71:14-16). You may decide to have praise songs playing in the background as you fall asleep at night, or put on music when you wake up first thing in the morning. You may decide to keep your radio dial on a Christian radio station and keep it on so that your home is continuously bathed in the hope of praise.

However you decide to offer your praise, dedicate a moment of each day to praise, even if it's only for five minutes. Praise lyrics and the act of worship will serve as a reminder of God's faithfulness.

My prayer for you: I pray that whatever you are struggling with, you will know that Jesus is right by your side. He loves you. He cares for you and wants to shower you with his healing and transforming love. I pray you will know that you can be honest with Jesus. And I pray your faith will grow as you learn to trust Jesus with your life and those of others. Amen.

3. WORRY

Whenever I received troubling news, I felt an instant ache in the pit of my stomach. The sudden urge to retch might sweep over me. Sometimes I cried. Sometimes a numb feeling of helplessness spilled into an outlook of hopelessness. It was not uncommon for me to lose patches of hair due to worry.

It was as if I found myself locked in a windowless room. In my search for a light switch, I grasped the air with my hands, grabbing onto anything that might give me a solid grounding. I felt steady for an instant, but I never gained a clear sense of my surroundings or how to get out of this room. Similarly, when difficult circumstances arose, I immediately called a friend, and received some comfort from these conversations, but before long, nervous energy presided over my thoughts and guided my actions. I felt helpless, weak—and anxious. Rarely did it occur to me to pray. If I did pray, my petitions were fleeting because I often hurried to figure out how I should fix my latest dilemma. Finally, I got to the point where I was weary of being shackled to these chains of worry, and I began my journey toward freedom by asking Jesus to help me break free from this emotional and spiritual bondage. One of the ways Jesus responded was to help me think about what my family taught me about worry.

My father is a worrier. Each week he worked a different shift, one week from six in the morning until two in the afternoon, the next week from two until ten at night, and the following week from ten until six the next morning. This almost soul-destroying routine defined my father's work experience for most of his life. It was not uncommon for him to catch snatches of sleep during the day before he started his shift, and then get up and cook us a meal because my mother was still at work.

I am deeply grateful that my father did not shirk his responsibility as a provider for our family, and I have the utmost respect for him as a parent. But I know that as a child, I learned how to worry by watching him fret about all kinds of issues. It is hard to pinpoint one particular predicament

that my father worried about because, as a child, it seemed to me he was anxious about everything and anything. I could not help seeing that his concerns for the welfare of our family burdened him. The pressures of his daily life caused worry to inch across his face and melancholy to frame his countenance. On more than one occasion, I saw him sit on the couch and lay the side of his head in the palm of his hand. When he sighed, sadness pervaded the room. My father never discussed financial matters or work experiences with my brother or me, but when he returned home from his shift, he carried the strain of his day like a laborer shouldering a sack of rocks.

My journey of learning to let go of worry and trust Jesus has not been easy or straightforward. But I have discovered the wisdom of reflecting on Jesus' words and teachings *before* the trials of life overwhelm me. I am learning that when I treasure Jesus' words in my heart, ruminate on the stories of his life, grapple with the textures and nuances of these narratives, and take stock of his teachings, I can temper the worry that threatens to rule my decisions and define my actions. The more open I am to the lessons of scripture, the more Jesus' words and actions shape my thinking, guide my choices, and equip me to respond to troubles that come my way. Envisioning myself calling out to Jesus in the midst of a storm—similar to the tempest that Jesus' disciples found themselves in—has enabled me to manage the symptoms of worry. I see Jesus walking across the rough seas toward me, his footsteps steady and assured. The rain tearing into the choppy seas and the brutal winds cannot sway his determination to get to me. And as he approaches, Jesus tells me not to worry. When he speaks, I am not afraid. When he rebukes the elements, the fierce winds cease, and Jesus quiets the stormy trials that have threatened to shake my faith in him. Other times, I imagine myself in the place of Jesus sleeping on a cushion in the stern of a boat, while a storm is raging. The softness of the cushion is warm against my skin. I snuggle into the brushed texture of its fabric. I am oblivious to the wrath of the storm. With Jesus by my side, I am completely at peace. His power fills me with hope and my confidence soars (see Mark 4:35-41).

Like Peter who put his faith in Jesus when he walked on the sea toward him, I find that when I look to Jesus, and am reliant on his wisdom, peace is mine. But when I consider the severe nature of my

troubles, and rely upon my own understanding of how to address my tribulations, I sink quickly into despondency just as Peter began to sink into the sea when he noticed the abrasive winds and became frightened (see Matthew 14:22-33).

Chronic worry sets up a vicious circle because worry has a tendency to produce more stress. Worry can drain us of energy and monopolize our thoughts with anxiety. Worry speaks of despair and discouragement. It is not in worry's best interest to console us, or reassure us with words of support, or robe us in peace, for its existence thrives on casting a shroud of gloom over our hardship.

What worries you? Has a particular worry so dominated your thoughts that you could think about nothing else? Have you gotten up in the middle of the night or woken up in a cold sweat thinking about it? Have you tried to address a problem only to find that no matter what you do, your troubles seem to get worse? Maybe you have found some temporary reprieves, but your worries keep eroding your sense of well-being. Are you sick of the steady diet of worry feeding your thoughts and actions?

The good news is that Jesus can help you prevent worry from ruling your life. Jesus will always speak words of encouragement into any adversity you encounter. His teachings envision hope. His language of love fosters contentment. Scripture offers some very practical ways of dealing with worry. Look to Jesus for guidance. Study what he does, become familiar with what he says, and notice how he addresses emotional and physical manifestations of worry.

Take a few minutes to picture this scene of one very concerned man:

Joseph, being a righteous man and unwilling to expose [Mary] to public dis-
grace, planned to dismiss her quietly. (Matthew 1:19)

He cannot shake his sadness. He loved her. No. He loves her. He
had asked her to be his wife, and she had accepted. So what happened? What caused her to . . . he cannot quite bring himself to
finish this course of questioning, and so he abandons his thoughts
to silence.

Uneasy with contemplation, worry voices its concerns: What
will people think? What will people say? How will you get out of
this dilemma with your reputation and integrity intact? How will
you explain this to your family? What will happen to Mary?

He sighs. He still loves her and is determined not to bring
any public humiliation upon her. She is too lovely, too good, too
kind to endure any form of attack on her character. He loves her,
but he cannot accept . . . again, his words disappear like daylight
eclipsed by a moonless night.

He sits down in grief and places his head into his hands. His
warm breath bathes his face. He does not know how long he
reflects in the womb of his pondering, but by the time he rises,
he has decided to dismiss her quietly, knowing that her departure
from his life will be like a shadow tracing his footsteps.

WHAT WILL THEY THINK?

Joseph, being a righteous man and unwilling to expose [Mary] to public disgrace, planned to dismiss her quietly. (Matthew 1:19)

We will never know if Joseph felt betrayed hurt, angry, or confused when he heard that his fiancé, Mary, was pregnant. He could have worried about what family members, friends, neighbors, and acquaintances would think. Or he could have been concerned that his reputation as an upstanding member of the community would be tarnished. He could have taken out his worries on Mary, or he could have abandoned her. He might have tried to gain sympathy as the wounded victim of betrayal. He could have had Mary publicly shamed or stoned.

But Joseph chose none of these paths. The Apostle Matthew tells us that Joseph was "unwilling to expose [Mary] to public disgrace." Joseph decided to go against the grain of the culture and not embrace the options of hurt or revenge. He found the strength to put aside what people might think. He was able to move beyond his private worries to public action of integrity.

How much do you worry about what other people think? How much do you find yourself trying to live up to other people's expectations? How much do you weigh other people's opinions when you make a decision? How important is their approval? Do you ever find yourself leading a double life, presenting yourself as a model Christian while trying to hide parts of yourself that need healing and understanding?

You do not have to live this way. Like Joseph, you can be free from other people's expectations and act out of integrity. Ask Jesus to transform your worries into thoughts and actions that speak of your faith in him. Ask Jesus to help you not be swayed by other people's expectations. If you find yourself cultivating a lifestyle of deception in your bid to please others, ask Jesus to help you surrender these practices to him. Ask him to help you live a life that pleases him and not everyone else.

PRAYER

Jesus, help me to submit my worries to you and allow you to shape my decisions and actions. Amen.

"DO NOT BE AFRAID"

"Joseph, son of David, do not be afraid to take Mary as your wife." (Matthew 1:20b)

We can imagine many reasons why Joseph might have been afraid to take Mary as his wife. He might have feared taking on the responsibility of caring for a woman who apparently was carrying another man's child. He might have been afraid of the stigma and possible shame that would stalk his family's life as people gossiped about Mary's predicament. Or he might have feared that people would think he had dishonored himself and Mary by consummating their union before they were married.

Any one of those reasons would have been enough to wake him at night with worry. But God met him in the midst of his anxieties, not by dismissing his apprehensions but by sending an angel to reassure him: "Do not be afraid . . . the virgin shall conceive and bear a son, and they shall name him Emmanuel, which means God is with us" (Matthew 1:20b, 23-24). With these words from God resounding in his dream, Joseph woke up and without delay did what the angel of the Lord commanded him to do.

Worry can cause our thoughts to chase all kinds of pessimistic scenarios around in our heads. We may try to consider all the possible outcomes. We may try to make sense out of things we do not understand. As our worries accumulate, fear can quickly consume us.

If you find yourself in a spot where your worry intensifies, think of Joseph. God did not reveal everything that would happen to him. Nor did God give him details about the struggles and triumphs he would face. And yet Joseph trusted God's message. Joseph believed what he heard.

Ask Jesus to help you believe what he promises in scripture. Ask him to help you fix your eyes on the One who is attentive to all the details in your life, even if you cannot see or sort them all out. As you learn to trust Jesus, you will know that he is with you at all times. As you trust in this truth, you can surrender your worries to him. Hear his words of assurance: "Do not be afraid."

PRAYER

Jesus, help me to trust you when I don't understand what's happening to me. Help me to not be afraid, but to believe in your promise that you will never leave or forsake me. Amen.

ONE THING WILL NOT CHANGE

Now after they had left, an angel of the Lord appeared to Joseph in a dream and said,
"Get up, take the child and his mother, and flee to Egypt, and remain there until I tell
you; for Herod is about to search for the child, to destroy him." (Matthew 2:13)

Joseph's worries about Mary were just the beginning. As if having to travel to Bethlehem and go through the birth in a stable were not enough, Joseph learned that King Herod wanted to kill all the newborns in the country in order to ensure that Jesus did not survive. God's angel warned Joseph in a dream to take his family to Egypt. Later, when it was safe, the angel directed them to return to the land of Israel.

This young family had to travel huge distances, over terrain that was sometimes difficult to cross, in weather that was not always kind. They journeyed to places where it was quite possible they did not know anyone. But like an ever-watchful parent, God knew that Joseph was worried about his family's safety, and God met him in his moments of anxiety. Joseph did not have to pretend that he knew how to handle every situation. He did not have to have all the answers. He did not always have to be strong. He was simply honest with God and did what God told him to do. And God was with this family every step of the way.

If you have relocated very often in your life, you know how difficult moving is. Any major change—from job shifts to relationship changes, from school transitions to births and deaths—can be hard, and it can cause great worry. But just as God guided Joseph and his family, Jesus wants to partner with you through it all. You do not need to have all the answers. You do not have to always "be strong." Jesus invites you to question and grapple with the problems you meet. But Jesus also invites you to make room for his love and provision.

Change will always be happening in your life. But one thing will not change: Jesus' faithfulness.

PRAYER

Jesus, help me to trust you when I have to make unexpected changes in my life. Help
me to live in the hope that is always available to me. Amen.

COME HOME

There he made his home in a town called Nazareth, so that what had been
spoken through the prophets might be fulfilled, "He will be called a Nazorean."
(Matthew 2:23)

After living in foreign countries, Joseph and his family eventually made their home in Nazareth. Perhaps by this stage of their faith journey, they had discovered a new definition of "home." Maybe they had come to understand that home was not so much a place as it was a state of trusting in the love and protection and provision of God. Did they know that their home was with Jesus?

Do you know and experience Jesus as "home"? Perhaps Jesus has guided you to places you did not want to go. Maybe his provisions have not looked like what you thought they ought to look like. Maybe you have been afraid. Coming to terms with change is not always easy. Perhaps you have been, or are, in predicaments you never expected to be or you worry each time you have to make an adjustment to something new.

Wherever you journey——whether to a new physical place, a new emotional place, or a new relationship——Jesus offers you the comfort of experiencing him as your home, for he will always be with you. Through it all, Jesus promises that you will never be alone. His love is enough to protect you from being dismayed by the forces of your everyday worries.

Embrace this truth: Your home, your resting place, your refuge from the storms of worry will always be in Jesus. No matter where he calls you to go, you will always be in the shelter of his presence.

PRAYER

Jesus, help me to experience your love as my home. Amen.

WHY WORRY?

"And can any of you by worrying add a single hour to your span of life?"
(Matthew 6:27)

Can worrying add a single hour to our lives? The glare of Jesus' question sheds light onto the futility of worrying. The answer resides in the question: Worry cannot add a single hour, minute, or even a fraction of a second to our lives. It can steal time from other activities and encroach upon the moments we spend with our loved ones. It can make us less attentive, less appreciative of the very things that could relieve our worry. Worry can also lead to disabling health problems when worry branches into more anxiety.

So why worry, Jesus asks. Jesus simply does not want us to be embroiled in this inadequate coping strategy.

Resisting the lure of worry and breaking away from this mode of negative thinking is a process. When you find yourself entering into this emotional wasteland, ask Jesus to help you trust and have faith in him. If you find yourself caught in a web of worries, don't be disheartened. Jesus can help you break the hold of worry from your life.

Ask yourself Jesus' question: "Can worrying add a single hour to my span of life?" Use scripture to help you slow down and stop the downward spiral of worry. Recall verses such as, "And those who know your name put their trust in you, for you, O LORD, have not forsaken those who seek you" (Psalm 9:10). Hold in your heart Jesus' healing words: "Look at the birds of the air; they neither sow nor reap nor gather into barns, and yet your heavenly Father feeds them. Are you not of more value than they?" (Matthew 6:26).

When worry begins to loom, Jesus can quell its rise and keep it from adding fuel to other troubled emotions, such as despair and hopelessness. Jesus is the great extinguisher of worry, for he is the giver of peace.

PRAYER

Jesus, thank you for understanding that I worry. Thank you for loving me enough to want to erase worry from my life. I want to receive the peace that can come only from you. Amen.

TRUE FREEDOM

"And why do you worry about clothing? Consider the lilies of the field, how they grow; they neither toil nor spin, yet I tell you, even Solomon in all his glory was not clothed like one of these. But if God so clothes the grass of the field, which is alive today and tomorrow is thrown into the oven, will he not much more clothe you—you of little faith? Therefore do not worry, saying, 'What will we eat?' or 'What will we drink?' or 'What will we wear?'. . . your heavenly Father knows that you need all these things. But strive first for the kingdom of God and his righteousness, and all these things will be given to you as well." (Matthew 6:28-33)

If there is any one word that describes our western society, it might be overconsumption—of food, of clothes, of the latest technology. We need clothes to wear, but how many do we need? We need food to eat, but how much is enough? Ironically, the things we think we need to satisfy us may end up being the very things that cause us the most worry. We may worry so much about owning or losing material possessions that our lives seem to lack purpose or meaning without them. We may get into so much debt trying to keep up with the latest trends that the stress level of maintaining our lifestyle breeds more worry.

Worry clouds our perspective and nurtures spiritual amnesia. Worry takes hold of our minds and causes us to forget that Jesus promises that his provision is enough.

The good news is that Jesus knows we need to be clothed, to be fed. He knows we need a place to live. He knows what burdens us. He understands how our worries can encroach upon our thoughts. Jesus acknowledges that we worry, even while he urges us not to worry.

Just as a potter skillfully shapes clay, Jesus can reshape our worries and mold them into faith in his provision. He promises us that God will provide for all our needs. And he reminds us that his words can feed our souls and satisfy our hunger for peace, love, and contentment.

The next time your worries threaten to take over, bring them to Jesus. Ask him to free you from your tangled thoughts and emotions. Ask him to renew your mind and replenish you in body and soul.

Ask him to teach you how to live in this freedom, so that in time you will be able to say:

> I have learned to be content with whatever I have. I know what it is to have little, and I know what it is to have plenty. In any and all circumstances I have learned the secret of being well-fed and of going hungry, or having plenty and of being in need. (Philippians 4:11-12)

PRAYER

Jesus, at times worry infiltrates my thoughts, motivates my decisions, and robs me of joy. Help me to live in the freedom of being content with your provision. Amen.

JUST AS I AM

Now as they went on their way, he entered a certain village, where a woman named Martha welcomed him into her home. She had a sister named Mary, who sat at the Lord's feet and listened to what he was saying. But Martha was distracted by her many tasks: so she came to him and asked, "Lord, do you not care that my sister has left me to do all the work by myself?" (Luke 10:38-40a)

It was common for people to welcome Jesus into their homes as he traveled from town to town teaching and healing and ministering. During one of these journeys, Jesus accepted Martha and Mary's invitation to stay in their home. Before long, Jesus began sharing his words of wisdom. Mary knelt by his feet and listened, but Martha busied herself with chores. For a while, all seemed to be fine, but something set Martha off. Maybe she fretted about how much work still needed to be done. Maybe she was worried about feeding a house full of people. Perhaps she began to be bothered that she was missing out on something important. Finally, she couldn't stand it any longer. Martha made her way to Jesus and expressed her frustration: "Lord, do you not care that my sister has left me to do all the work by myself?"

Many biblical scholars have drawn many conclusions from this text. But for those of us who worry, one thing comes through loud and clear: Martha did not hide the state of mind she was in. She did not pretend to be anything other than who she was. She did not try to filter her feelings or hide her frustration.

Take this interaction between Martha and Jesus to heart. You, too, can approach Jesus without having to edit your feelings. Your worries will not overwhelm Jesus—even if you have brought the same worries to him over and over again. Just as he listened to Martha's complaints, so will he be there to listen to you.

PRAYER

Jesus, I am thankful that I can come to you just as I am. Thank you for hearing me. Thank you for taking my concerns seriously. Amen.

CHOOSE WHAT IS BETTER

"Tell her then to help me." But the Lord answered her, "Martha, Martha, you are worried and distracted by many things; there is need of only one thing. Mary has chosen the better part, which will not be taken away from her."(Luke 10:40b-42)

Did Jesus care about Martha's worries and frustration? The answer is found in his response. He did not dismiss or minimize her feelings. He acknowledged that she was worried and did not put a stop to the flow of her objections.

Instead, Jesus called her by name—twice. "Martha, Martha." His deliberate repetition of her name suggests that he knew her well and hints at his compassion for her. It suggests that she had his full attention. Jesus understood that Martha was disappointed, that Mary did not meet her expectations.

If you are ever tempted to think that Jesus is tired of listening to your concerns, or that your worries are too small to bother him with, think of his response to Martha. Jesus knows you, too, by name. He holds you in great compassion. He takes your problems seriously.

But he might not respond in just the way you planned or hoped. For although Jesus considered Martha's request, he did not order Mary to help her. Instead, he lovingly told Martha, "You are worried and distracted by many things. There is need of only one thing. Mary has chosen the better part." When Jesus listens, he can take you beyond the feelings you are entangled in and show you a more excellent way.

Let Jesus' words encourage you. When you feel overwhelmed by worries and distractions, when you feel frustrated that the people you expect to help you do not seem to be anywhere around, ask Jesus, "What is 'the better part' that 'will not be taken away' from me?" Then listen carefully to what Jesus has to say to you.

PRAYER

Jesus, thank you for calling me by name. Thank you for listening to my worries. Help me to see that you have better things in mind for me. Amen.

ANOTHER ALTERNATIVE

When it grew late, his disciples came to him and said, "This is a deserted place, and the hour is now very late; send them away so that they may go into the surrounding country and villages and buy something for themselves to eat. But he answered them, "You give them something to eat." They said to him, "Are we to go and buy two hundred denarii worth of bread, and give it to them to eat?" (Mark 6:35-37)

Jesus had probably been teaching a good part of the day, and evening had started to drape the sky. The disciples were beginning to get worried. Here they were in this remote place, surrounded by thousands of people who were in need of a meal. Mobilizing everyone and directing them to the surrounding country and villages to find dinner seemed like the only thing to do, but was a logistical nightmare. Where could this many people go? Could the food sellers in the neighboring areas supply such a large quantity of food? Who was going to pay for it?

Like most people who are feeling anxious, the disciples tried to think through the alternatives and get the situation under control. Rather than ask Jesus what they should do, they instructed Jesus what he ought to tell his followers.

Jesus did not ignore their instruction, nor did he reprimand them for telling him what to do. Instead, he responded to their demand by suggesting another alternative: "You give them something to eat."

The disciples' defensive response to Jesus' proposal reflects their frustration and genuine confusion: "Are we to go and buy two hundred denarii worth of bread, and give it to them to eat?" Their question gives us a few clues about how worried they really were. For starters, they had already calculated out how much money would be needed to pay for enough food to feed the hungry crowd. They also seem to have wrestled with the idea of having to give food to so many people. Ultimately, their worry over the cost and amount of bread that had to be purchased eclipsed their original concern about the followers going hungry.

Do you recognize any of this behavior? Have you been in a quandry when it seemed up to you to solve the problem, when there seemed to be no one else to take care of things, so it was up to you?

Take special note of this exchange between Jesus and his disciples. You might try the disciples' approach and tell Jesus exactly how he ought to address a particular matter. Or you could simply ask Jesus how you should respond to the matter at hand. Either way, Jesus might offer you another alternative. Are you prepared to listen to what he has to say? Are you willing to let go of your strategic plans and act upon his instructions?

PRAYER

Jesus, teach me that I can come to you without having everything all figured out. Help me to be able to hear your instructions and act on your words. Amen.

THE GREAT PROVIDER

*And he said to them, "How many loaves have you? Go and see." When they had
found out, they said, "Five, and two fish." Then he ordered them to get all the
people to sit down in groups on the green grass. So they sat down in groups of
hundreds and of fifties. Taking the five loaves and the two fish, he looked up to
heaven, and blessed and broke the loaves, and gave them to his disciples to set
before the people; and he divided the two fish among them all. And all ate and
were filled. (Mark 6:38-42)*

Jesus did not ask the disciples to speculate about how much food they
thought was available. He told them to go and see for themselves how
many loaves there were. They returned with even more than they had
been sent to find: five loaves *plus* two fish. This may seem like a minor
detail, but for those of us who worry——especially about whether there
will be "enough"——finding more than we expected is a wonderful surprise. We can smile at Jesus' subtle humor in this already seemingly
impossible situation.

Then Jesus looked up to heaven and blessed these humble gifts, acknowledging God as the great provider. And absolutely everyone was fed.

How many times do you fear that what is available is not enough? Or
worry that there is no way that the task at hand can get done? Or believe
that you are the only one who is struggling with a particular issue and no
one else could possibly understand?

Jesus is attentive to your every need. His wisdom surpasses all others. His provision is enough. He may lead you to others who will teach
you about sharing. He may allow you the surprise of finding more than
you expected. Whatever he gives you will be just what you need.

PRAYER

*Jesus, thank you that you want to take care of my every need. Help me to be grateful
for your provision. Amen.*

THE CUSHION

A great windstorm arose, and the waves beat into the boat, so that the boat was already being swamped. But he was in the stern, asleep on the cushion; and they woke him up and said to him, "Teacher, do you not care that we are perishing?" (Mark 4:37-38)

Even as the storm raged, causing the waves to saturate the boat, Jesus slept in the stern on a cushion. If he felt the boat being tossed every which way by the harsh weather, he did not let it interrupt his slumber. Compelled by worry, his disciples woke Jesus up and asked him "Teacher, do you not care that we are perishing?"

Jesus did not answer them, but instead, got up and issued the following order to the sea: "Peace! Be still" (Mark 4:39b). The sea submitted to Jesus' authority, and "the wind ceased, and there was a dead calm" (Mark 4:39d). Only after the environment was completely settled in a peaceful lull did Jesus verbally address the disciples' worried question, "Teacher, do you not care . . ." But rather than answering directly, he responded with more questions: "Why are you afraid? Have you still no faith?" (Mark 4:40).

They did not reply, but instead "were filled with great awe and said to one another, 'Who then is this, that even the wind and the sea obey him?'" (Mark 4:41b).

Jesus is our cushion from the wrath of the storm. Jesus cushions us from being subdued by the worries of our everyday lives. When we learn to trust him, when we learn to be in awe of his power and strength, our faith acts as a buttress against the force of whatever worrisome situation we encounter.

Jesus cares for you. It matters to Jesus when you are perishing in your worries. There is hope. You, too, can find solace in his presence because no person or thing is mightier than Jesus. So rather than let worry batter your belief in Jesus' strength, allow Jesus to help you rest in his protection.

PRAYER

Jesus, help me not to be worried when an unexpected trial comes my way, but to embrace and rest in your awesome power. Thank you that even the wind and the sea obey you. Amen.

MANAGING WORRY

The following guidelines offer some ways to help you make peace with worrying thoughts. Ask Jesus to help you decide which strategies will be of use to you. Be open to the possibility that Jesus can free you from the worries that entangle you.

1. Be honest with Jesus. *Tell Jesus the specific nature of your worries. Don't withhold anything from him.*

Remember that Martha did not mince her words when she approached Jesus with her concerns, and Jesus was not overwhelmed by her distress. Jesus *wants* to lift your burdens and soothe your tensions. He *wants* to hear about everything you struggle with. There is no emotion or worry he cannot handle. If you are filled with questions, or anger, or despair, he can handle it. And if he does not appear to be responding, if he seems distant or silent, continue to dialogue with him. Talk to him silently or aloud. Converse with him in the same way you would have a conversation with a friend. The most important thing is to keep on sharing your innermost thoughts.

The second important thing is to bring your distress to Jesus right away. If you allow your worries and deliberations to take root in your mind, your problems can begin to escalate to the point where you will not be able to see how Jesus could possibly help.

Trying to avoid what's bothering you is like attempting to block out any sights or sounds by putting your hands over your ears, singing aloud, and closing your eyes. No matter how hard you try, you cannot keep this posture forever, and the timbres and visual reminders of your problems will come flooding in.

Jesus is not asking you to hide from your problems or delude yourself into thinking they do not exist. Neither is he asking you to pretend that you are not worried or afraid. He is asking you to believe in him and rely on his wisdom to get you through the difficult things you face.

Consider him who endured such hostility against himself from sinners, so that you may not grow weary or lose heart. (Hebrews 12:3)

2. Confess your sins. *You may find that some of your worries stem from making poor choices. Bring your shortcomings to Jesus.*

Jesus waits patiently for you to be honest with him about your struggles. When you tell him about the poor choices or unwise decisions you have made, he will not badger or shame or disrespect or ridicule you. But if you keep your troubles from him, your sense of isolation and loneliness will be compounded. You can become even more immersed in worries, and anguish can become even more of a companion in your life.

Letting go of the behaviors and thoughts that have contributed to your worries may not be easy; it may even be painful. But Jesus will always offer you forgiveness, embrace you with grace, and pour out his mercy on you.

Hold on to Jesus' promise: "Friend, your sins are forgiven" (Luke 5:20b).

3. Claim your identity in God. *Your name is not "worry." Some of the names God has bestowed upon you include "loved by God" (John 3:16), "precious" (Isaiah 43:4), and "child of God" (1 John 4:4), and as his sons and daughters you are "inscribed in the palms of God's hand" (Isaiah 49:16). God calls you by name (Isaiah 43:1e). Jesus calls you "friend" (John 15:15), and as God's Beloved, Jesus loves you (1 John 4:7-16).*

It is significant that God called Jesus his Beloved *before* Jesus entered into full-time ministry. This expression of affirmation illustrates that God's love is not dependent on what we do. God's love is an unshakeable foundation. Claiming our identity in Jesus is key to alleviating the scourge of worry from our lives.

Here is one tangible way to anchor your mind in God's love: Put your name or the personal pronoun "I" or "me" into a specific passage of scripture that addresses your circumstances. For instance, change the scripture that reads "You are my Son, the Beloved; with you I am well pleased" (Mark 1:11b) to "[Your name], you are my Beloved daughter [or son], and I am so pleased with you." Or simply, "I am God's son [or daughter], the Beloved, and God is pleased with me."

Say out aloud, "In the name of Jesus, I will not allow my circumstances to have control of my life. I am God's child, I am not orphaned. Jesus is my strength and deliverer."

"I will not leave you orphaned; I am coming to you. In a little while the world will no longer see me, but you will see me; because I live, you also will live. On that day you will know that I am in my Father, and you in me, and I in you."(John 14:18-20)

4. Read scripture. *If you are consumed by worry, choosing to take time to read scripture may be one of the more difficult things to do. And yet, scripture can remind you that Jesus is by your side every step of the way.*

Try this strategy that is inspired by the Benedictine approach to engaging with scripture: After reading a section of scripture, ask Jesus to draw your attention to a word or a verse that speaks to your predicament. Then take your time and slowly say these words to yourself. Pause for a little while and allow Jesus to speak to you through these words.

Another strategy is to re-enact a portion of scripture in your mind. For instance, in Matthew 19:14-15 Jesus says: "'Let the little children come me, and do not stop them; for it is to such as these that the kingdom of heaven belongs.' And he laid his hands on them and went on his way." After reading this scripture, close your eyes, and imagine Jesus gently holding you as a child in his arms and praying for you.

When words of worry try to tell you that you are alone or that your situation is hopeless, reflect on God's word. Reading scripture the first thing in the morning and before you go to bed at night can remind you of Jesus' faithfulness and put your mind at ease. Just as Jesus told the storms to be still, so you can lean on Jesus and, by his power, tell the storms of your life to be still.

Rejoice in the Lord always; again I will say, Rejoice. Let your gentleness be known to everyone. The Lord is near. Do not worry about anything, but in everything by prayer and supplication with thanksgiving let your requests be made known to God. And the peace of God, which surpasses all understanding, will guard your hearts and your minds in Christ Jesus. (Philippians 4:4-7)

5. Worship and praise. *Worshiping God and proclaiming his power through praise can remind you that there is no worrisome predicament that Jesus cannot help you overcome.*

Sometimes it is very difficult to worship God when worry shapes your thoughts. Singing to God when you are struggling may seem like a strange practice. Ultimately, though, the praise is not about you; it is about God. Even if there seems to be nothing in your present life to praise God for, praise God for what he has done in the past. Praise God for giving you life and for being the creator of all things. Like David you can declare "For it was you who formed my inward parts; you knit me together in my mother's womb. I praise you, for I am fearfully and wonderfully made. Wonderful are your works; that I know very well" (Psalm 139:13-14). Praise God for loving all humanity, for being faithful, for providing for you and giving you your "daily bread" (Matthew 6:11). Praise God for desiring that you live a life where you can proclaim, "You prepare a table before me in the presence of my enemies; you anoint my head with oil; my cup overflows. Surely goodness and mercy shall follow me all the days of my life, and I shall dwell in the house of the LORD my whole life long" (Psalm 23:5-6).

God invites you to find liberation from worry in the life-giving power of praise. You can shout your praise with a loud voice because "When the righteous cry for help, the LORD hears, and rescues them from all their troubles. The LORD is near to the brokenhearted, and saves the crushed in spirit. Many are the afflictions of the righteous, but the LORD rescues them from them all" (Psalm 34:17-19). You can relax in a chair and shut your eyes because "The counsel of the LORD stands forever, the thoughts of his heart to all generations" (Psalm 33:11). You can dance and rejoice in a God who "is our help and shield" (Psalm 33:20b).

Within time, you will experience the benefits of nurturing a lifestyle of praise. Jesus' wisdom can calm your worries. The more you praise God, continue to reflect upon Jesus' character, and consider his trustworthiness, the more you will receive God's peace. When you praise God, know that hope rather than worry will occupy your heart, shape your thoughts, and underscore your actions. Rest in the serenity that comes with Jesus' promise that "your Father knows what you need before you ask him" (Matthew 6:8b).

Finally, beloved, whatever is true, whatever is honorable, whatever is just, whatever is pure, whatever is pleasing, whatever is commendable, if there is any excellence and if there is anything worthy of praise, think about these things. Keep on doing the things that you have learned and received and heard and seen in me, and the God of peace will be with you. (Philippians 4:8-9)

6. Seek help. *If worry becomes a persistent way of being, consider seeking professional counseling. Ask others to pray for you and offer their emotional support.*

If worry seems to envelop your life, there is no shame in looking for partnership. We all need others to support us and serve us in and out of our time of need. Ask Jesus to help you discern if counseling or some form of medical assistance would be beneficial as you work to overcome the problems you are dealing with. Ask him to lead you to a few trusted individuals who will pray for you, offer encouragement, and other means of practical help.

7. Don't worry about those circumstances that are beyond your control. *When circumstances happen that are beyond your control, release your worry to Jesus and move forward by praying and asking him how you should respond to the situation you are facing.*

You can save yourself from a lot of worry when you recognize that you cannot go back and undo a situation that has already unfolded; you can only go forward. Jairus could not change the fact that his daughter had fallen ill, but he could ask Jesus to help heal her (see Mark 5:21-43). You, too, can ask Jesus to give you a sense of hope that, no matter what has happened, Jesus' provision, his love for you, his power will enable you to overcome trying seasons. Hope in Jesus will help you transcend your worries and enable you to see your present and future through the wisdom that one thing will never change—Jesus' faithfulness.

When you are baffled by events beyond your control, these are the times when you need to rely not on what you feel or on what you perceive about your situation, but on what Jesus promises: "The prayer of the righteous is powerful and effective" (James 5:16c). As hard as it might be, keep the channels of prayer open. Don't make decisions

without praying for Jesus' wisdom. Don't rely on your own understanding (Proverbs 3:5-8).

Worry has a tendency to block out memories of Jesus' faithfulness. It might be useful to keep a blessings journal as a form of prayer. Each day, ask Jesus to help you recall several moments that were blessings. Write these reflections in a journal so when the symptoms of worry begin to surface, you can read these entries and be reminded of how Jesus has met your needs. By documenting the times Jesus has come through for you, you can learn to trust in the truth that "Jesus Christ is the same yesterday and today and forever" (Hebrews 13:8).

My prayer for you: I pray that you will experience how Jesus can love and care for you through the emotional storms of worry. It is my prayer that you will allow Jesus to free you from the crippling symptoms of worry with his profound and unmatchable wisdom. Amen.

---

4. JEALOUSY

He could not quite pinpoint when these feelings had begun, but for many years a kernel of envy nested in his thoughts. No matter how much he willed them to subside, no matter how much he did not want to admit it to himself, these thoughts of jealousy kept on festering in his mind.

How could he feel jealous about someone he loved like a brother? They had been buddies since they were seven years old. They played football together. They imagined make-believe worlds where they pretended to be pirates, soldiers, cowboys, and explorers. They developed an ultra top-secret whistle call to signal each other. They even invented their own language and took great pride in knowing that no one could break their code. With these recollections, he smiled at how seriously they had applied themselves to such activities.

When they graduated from college and started their first jobs, they applauded one another's achievements. They attended each other's weddings and celebrated the births of their children. And during the difficult seasons of life, they had been each other's rock.

He could not deny that a part of him wished the very best for his friend. Some moments he genuinely delighted in his friend's successes. But he began to notice that whenever his friend told him about his latest promotion, though he smiled and feigned delight in his friend's good fortune, deep down, he resented those stories of achievement. The first time his friend failed to achieve a goal, he was surprised by the euphoria he felt; now such feelings had become a mainstay in his thoughts. He disliked himself for finding it difficult to be happy for his friend's achievements, and he carried this guilt wherever he went. He could not seem to shake his conflicting, contradictory——even ugly——thoughts about his friend.

Now as they settled into the latter part of their middle age, it was hard for him to come to terms with the fact that his friend no longer depended on him in the way that he used to. At the same time, on those now rare occasions when his friend showed signs of needing his help, a

bile of annoyance rose within him because he did not want to expend time and energy bailing his friend out from his troubles.

Jealousy spoke clearly to his inner thoughts during these moments: Haven't you come to your friend's aid at the expense of sacrificing your own dreams? While you offer yourself and your life on the altar of friendship, your friend will continue to prosper. If you have any sense, you will distance yourself from him. If you know what's good for you, you will withhold any information that might help him realize his aspirations. That way, you can be sure he will not experience greater accomplishments in his life.

Beneath these jealous musings lay another persistent question that refused to go away: Had it become easier for him to help his friend because he did not want to face his own problems? This question proved to be the hardest to come to terms with because it opened up a floodgate of other questions that he would rather have avoided: Had he really formulated any tangible dreams of his own? Or had he been living a life that others had expected him to live?

His parents raised him to believe that he would be the one others would want to model themselves after. His family recognized early on that he was academically gifted, and they made sure that he attended the best schools. Whenever he applied himself to a subject that interested him, he excelled, but many years had passed since those early academic accomplishments, and it had been a while since he had enjoyed any considerable professional success. Now, as much as he hated to admit it, he was fearful of not being everything that he had built himself up to be. He was afraid of failing, and the thought embarrassed him. Yet he despised people feeling sorry for him, and his pride rejected any hint of pity. And so, little by little, he withdrew from the game of excelling. To utter the words that he was unhappy was foreign to him, but he could not get rid of the sadness suffocating his life.

And so he carefully assembled a life of adult make-believe. He tried to be a good friend to everyone he met. He greeted his friends with a pat on the back and always had a word of encouragement for them. He fished with his buddies and knew how to tell a good joke. He could engineer a robust conversation about politics, but because of his tact of

diplomacy, he somehow offended no one. He always seemed to have answers to every question posed to him. He showed little to no sign of emotional weakness. He dutifully went to church each Sunday and became a member of the board of trustees.

For the most part, he presented a positive front at home. He paid the bills. He attended his children's sports games and congratulated them on their academic achievements. He earned enough money so his wife could buy the things she wanted. Still, his attempts to maintain this picture of domestic bliss were threatened whenever one of his children wanted to share their troubles with him. Similarly, whenever his wife tried to express her unhappiness about the state of their marriage, a quick stare or a silent pause of dismissal quickly submerged such sentiments into an uneasy truce of denial.

Gradually, the strain of managing this lifestyle of adult make-believe began to take its toll. He found it hard to sleep at night. He was often restless, and when he was alone, despondency slowly crept in because his fear of failing continued to haunt him. When he looked at his friend who seemed to be doing so well, he smothered his fear in jealousy. It was not so much what he said to his friend that was revealing, but what he did not say that clouded their friendship. Even when his friend's boasts of success became little more than a screen to camouflage mounting debt, it did not change anything because envy had now found a resting place in his mind. His heart had become callused.

Scripture does not shy away from the travesty of jealousy, and this is especially apparent in the story of John the Baptist. John the Baptist was not rich. He did not hold a high status in society. He did not court the approval of the privileged elite. But his reputation as a follower of God, his willingness to serve God by baptizing all those who wanted to confess and repent of their sins, spread throughout the land. And many were threatened by his ability to draw people to Jesus——even the king. Even with all his wealth and power, jealousy could well have motivated King Herod's decision to have John imprisoned. Why would a king who had money, political influence, and the devotion of many be jealous of a man who ate locusts and wore clothing made of camel hair? The answer lies not so much with John the Baptist, but in the one whom he followed——Jesus.

King Herod feared Jesus and envied his power. And it was this more than anything else that ate away at him, erupting in jealousy and driving him eventually to agree to John the Baptist's death.

For those of us who struggle with jealous thoughts, there is good news. Jesus understands that when we wrestle with this emotion, jealously penetrates our decision-making, distorting our perception of others. He wants to release us from jealousy's grip. Confessing our jealous thoughts to Jesus is a start because it prevents these feelings from becoming established in our hearts. But overcoming jealous thoughts is a daily challenge that requires us to be continually honest with Jesus about our feelings. Asking Jesus to help us love one another as he loved us is the key to rising above jealousy. When we can respond to others with thoughts and actions underscored by his love, we will be free from the bondage of jealousy.

Give yourself a few minutes to picture
the disciples' struggle with jealousy:

Then they came to Capernaum; and when he was in the house he asked them,
"What were you arguing about on the way?" But they were silent, for on the
way they had argued with one another who was the greatest. (Mark 9:33-34)

It starts out as just a simple banter among friends, but it quickly
turns into a full-scale argument. One of them begins to boast
about his teaching abilities. Another brings up how many people he has healed. Someone else describes how he commanded
demons to leave. Another declares that Jesus loves him the most.
Before they know it, each is trying to convince the other that he
deserves the title of the greatest.

In bullish vigor, one man's words charge the red cloth of
another's assertions. With a slight turn of a phrase, another disciple lifts the red cloth of his opinions high into the air, egging the
others to unleash more arguments. Their raging words are like
stomping bulls causing a cloud of dust to rise, polluting the air.

There is a moment of pause before their arguments peak.
Their pronouncements thicken the air, as they ready themselves
to stampede into another slew of verbal insults. Jealousy floods
their thoughts, and the taste of anger veils their tongues as they
attack once again. By the end, each point of view is so fierce that
their convictions have left multiple stab wounds.

Captivated by their own sense of themselves, enamored
with their prowess to parlay their gifts in the world, the disciples
are entangled in the web of their own insights, their own glory,
their own perception of themselves. And Jesus is nowhere to be
found.

EMBARRASSED TO SILENCE

Then they came to Capernaum; and when he was in the house he asked them,
"What were you arguing about on the way?" But they were silent, for on the way
they had argued with one another who was the greatest. (Mark 9:33-34)

It was probably the last thing the disciples wanted Jesus to know. They had
been arguing amongst themselves about who was the greatest. In heated
conversation, they had vied to assert their right to claim such a mantle
of stature. They were a tight-knit group and probably shared most everything with each other, but their jealousy had gotten the best of them. It
was as if they had locked themselves in a room where every inch of floor,
wall, and ceiling space was pasted with cracked mirrors. When the disciples looked at each other, they saw themselves in each other's fragmented
image, and Jesus was nowhere to be found in their reflection.

Then Jesus asked the very question they hadn't wanted him to ask:
"What were you arguing about?" Maybe out of his love for them Jesus
wanted to know what caused such friction. Perhaps he wanted to temper
their dispute or to be included in their discussion. Maybe he wanted to
heal their wounded pride.

But no one said a word. Jesus' question sat loudly in their embarrassed silence. The disciples' unwillingness to bring Jesus into their debate
reveals something about the nature of their self-promotion and self-con-
gratulatory behavior—and the underlying jealousies that launched their
argument.

Jealousy can be an embarrassing emotion. It is not something we
want to tell others about. But when we find ourselves avoiding Jesus,
hoping he will not ask us about something, it is a signal that this is the very
time we need to share our thoughts with him.

When you have jealous thoughts that you are ashamed to share with
Jesus, when you do something out of jealousy that you do not want him
to know about, it is important to know that Jesus waits patiently for you
to come to him. He wants you to share every aspect of your life with
him. He will not badger you. He will not cringe or be shocked by your
thoughts and actions. His love will not shy away from you. His love will

always beckon you to move toward him. He is waiting to free you from the vice of jealously.

Turning away from Jesus will always invite bondage to the very thoughts and actions you detest in yourself.

Turning to Jesus will always bring freedom.

PRAYER

Jesus, thank you that your love longs for me to come to you. Thank you that there is nothing that I cannot share with you. Help me to be more like you and live a life of humility. Amen.

A DIFFERENT STANDARD

He sat down, called the twelve, and said to them, "Whoever wants to be first must be last of all and servant of all." (Mark 9:35)

When met with the disciples' silence, Jesus did not judge them or force them to give an account of what they had been discussing. Instead, he simply took a seat and called the twelve to him, saying, "Whoever wants to be first must be last of all and servant of all."

This teaching goes against the grain of what our culture prescribes as the road to success. It is antithetical to highly developed strategies meant to ensure that we will come out on top—in business, in school, in sports, in elections, in any arena of life.

Depending on what our aspirations are, we may be inspired by Jesus' words—or hear them as criticism that will deter us from achieving what we want to accomplish. For the person who strives to be first, to be considered number one by their peers, success by any other standard may be difficult to accept. For those who have little to no expectations for their lives and have never considered themselves the sort who would ever be first, the notion of being last may be an all-too-familiar occurrence.

Jesus' words apply equally to us all: to those who expect to be treated as if they are special, and to those who expect to be last. For Jesus is talking about a different kind of success, a different kind of standard. He envisions us living in freedom from the world's expectations, free from jealously about what others have.

For both the overachiever and the underachiever, jealously is a complicated and crippling emotion. Jealousy surfaces out of a place of fear. Jealousy can make us feel afraid that someone will take our place in somebody's affections. Jealousy can make us want to demean others, or discredit them, or actively hinder their potential to succeed. Jealousy can keep us from building close relationships of support and cooperation. Jealousy can foster hate.

If jealousy shadows your thoughts, Jesus can free you. Jesus, who had a seat at the right hand of God, could have asked for anything, and yet he chose to be last of all. He did not insist on his right to be first. He did

not elevate himself above others. He did not fight to get the attention of others. Jesus was content to yield to God's authority; he was willing to submit to God's leading. He became our servant.

Jesus wants to serve you. He yearns to embrace you in his love, to give you rest in the safety of his arms. Take comfort that his love puts each person first and surrender your jealous thoughts to him. Receive his love so you can work in solidarity with others, not in opposition.

PRAYER

Jesus, thank you that you set a different standard than the world does. Teach me how to care for those you have put in my path and help me to rest in your love. Amen.

THE ARMS OF LOVE

Then he took a child and put it among them; and taking it in his arms, he said to them, "Whoever welcomes one such child in my name welcomes me, and whoever welcomes me welcomes not me but the one who sent me." (Mark 9:36-37)

When Jesus took a child into his arms, his act of love was unconditional. He did not wait for the child to be in a certain frame of mind nor did he expect anything in return. He simply welcomed this child into his loving embrace.

That is how God receives us. In God's eyes, we are all children whom he loves, regardless of our gender, ethnicity, age, socio-economic background, looks, intelligence, or abilities. We are created in the image of God, and Jesus claims us as God's Beloved. Just as Jesus took one child into his arms, God loves each of us one by one. That is what it means to serve others: to love one person at a time, in Jesus' name.

The path of love is the essence of freedom from jealousy.

If there are areas of your life where you are feeling unloved, these are the places where jealousy can arise and cause you to direct your feelings of inadequacy toward others. The good news is that you can run into Jesus' arms and allow his love to wrap around you. Allow him to comfort you so your feelings of jealousy are quieted. Let his attentiveness help you overcome your need to envy what others have.

His love will listen to your jealous feelings and enable you to release them. His love is enough to quiet the despondency in your heart and turn your jealousy into a hope that transcends your suspicions or fears about others.

PRAYER

Jesus, teach me to be like a child who is receptive to your teachings. Hold me in your love so I won't need to hold others in jealousy. Amen.

LOVE CONQUERS JEALOUSY

And as he sat at dinner in Levi's house, many tax collectors and sinners were also sitting with Jesus and his disciples —for there were many who followed him. When the scribes of the Pharisees saw that he was eating with sinners and tax collectors, they said to his disciples, "Why does he eat with tax collectors and sinners?"(Mark 2:15-16)

After Levi the tax collector accepted Jesus' invitation to become a follower, he invited Jesus to come to his home for dinner—along with a few of his tax collector friends and other acquaintances. If thoughts of jealousy had ruled in Levi's heart, he would have kept Jesus to himself and prevented others from getting close. But because the love of Jesus was in his heart, there was no room for envy. He wanted his friends to get to know Jesus.

This is how love conquers jealousy.

But the scribes of the Pharisees who witnessed this event were not happy with Jesus' choice of companions. When they noticed the people surrounding Jesus, they turned to the disciples and asked why Jesus was eating with these "sinners." The scribes had already dismissed the tax collectors as undesirable members of society, and they questioned Jesus' wisdom in even associating with them.

If you struggle with jealousy, take comfort in the knowledge that Jesus treats all people equally. He does not seek the approval of others about how he should love you. He will always treat you as one of God's beloved children. No matter what the world says about you, no matter who rejects you, no matter what others think about you, you can always be assured that Jesus wants to be with you.

Ask Jesus to teach you to follow the examples of the "sinners" who found contentment in Jesus' presence.

PRAYER

Jesus, thank you that I will always be a priority in your love. Help me to live in the fullness of your love and release me from the bondage of jealousy. Amen.

THROUGH THE EYES OF LOVE

"Why does he eat with tax collectors and sinners?"(Mark 2:16b)

The scribes who questioned Jesus were learned men and religious leaders, and yet they did not understand Jesus. They were well-versed in religious law, but they did not have all the answers. Quite possibly they felt justified, as gatekeepers of the faith, to judge Jesus' actions. They probably saw themselves as superior to the more despised elements of society. But underneath it all, they felt threatened. They were not so much envious of the people who were invited to eat with Jesus, but jealous of Jesus' popularity and power.

Notice that they did not broach their question to Jesus, but to the disciples. Their actions expose the underbelly of jealousy: Jealousy has a tendency to flourish in the shadows of our thoughts and to direct our attention away from our own insecurities. As a result, we can become overly involved or captivated by the motives and intentions of others.

At times you may find it easier to look down on someone than to try to understand them—or love them. The same false pride that drove the scribes may be masking the darker emotion of jealousy. Jealousy does not celebrate the achievements and good fortune of others. Jealousy does not take stock of the miracle of love that Jesus lavishes upon others. Rather, jealously looks for a way to put other people down. The worse they look, the better you look.

If left unchecked, jealousy will not only rob you of joy in your relationships but will also deepen your dissatisfaction with yourself—and cause you to turn your back on the love and commandments of Jesus.

The challenge is to allow Jesus to shape your opinions of others. Ask Jesus to search your motives. Let his wisdom and teachings transform your thoughts. Ask him to open your eyes to see people through his love.

Allowing Jesus to change your beliefs and viewpoints about others will not always be easy, but it is necessary if you want to follow his commandment to love others. Ask Jesus for the humility to put this petition into practice:

Search me, O God, and know my heart;
test me and know my thoughts.
See if there is any wicked way in me
and lead me in the way everlasting. (Psalm 139:23-24)

PRAYER

Jesus, reveal to me the ways in which my thoughts are hurtful to you. Help me to live in the fullness of your love and to love others out of your pure love. Amen.

NUMBER ONE PRIORITY

When John heard in prison what the Messiah was doing, he sent word by his disciples and said to him, "Are you the one who is to come, or are we to wait for another?" (Matthew 11:2-3)

We can learn a lot about jealousy——or, more accurately, the absence of it——from John the Baptist. So devoted was he to God's call that the material artifacts of the world held little appeal to him. He shunned status and position, and chose to live a life of humble servitude while wearing "clothing of camel's hair with a leather belt around his waist" and eating "locusts and wild honey" (Matthew 3:4).

When a crowd of followers questioned whether John might be the Messiah, he responded by saying, "I baptize you with water; but one who is more powerful than I is coming; I am not worthy to untie the thong of his sandals" (Luke 3:16b).

Rather than showing any sign of competing with Jesus, John championed the perspective that there was no one greater than Jesus. At no time did John court the approval or accolade of others. His source of contentment stemmed from following God's instructions, baptizing all who came to repent of their sins.

When the authorities threw John into prison for his actions, rather than bemoaning his situation, he sent his disciples to find out whether Jesus was the Messiah he had been waiting for. His question, "Are you the one?" revealed his hunger to be in the presence of the Messiah.

It did not occur to John to claim credit for his own acts of service or to be jealous of Jesus. John's message made no mention of his accomplishments in ministry. He only desired to know whether the Messiah had come to earth and God's promise to the world had come to fruition. John's attention on God's hope for the coming of Jesus never wavered.

In poetic prose John promised his followers, "He will baptize you with the Holy Spirit and fire. His winnowing fork is in his hand, to clear his threshing floor and to gather the wheat into his granary; but the chaff he will burn with unquenchable fire" (Luke 3:16c-17).

Jesus can sift the chaff of jealousy and "burn" its influence out of your life. He can also invite you to enjoy the harvest of his love by teaching you to make decisions that are gathered from the endlessly abundant "granary" of his wisdom. Ask Jesus to reveal himself to you as your Messiah. Ask him to teach you how to make him your number one priority. As you look to him, jealousy will have less and less hold on your thoughts and actions. So like John the Baptist you can joyfully say, "My joy has been fulfilled. [Jesus] must increase, but I must decrease" (John 3:29d-30).

PRAYER

Jesus, no matter what I face, help me to live in the hope and peace that comes from knowing and experiencing that you are the Messiah. Help me to hunger for the fruit of love that can only come from you and to relinquish to you my thoughts of jealousy. Amen.

CREATED FOR PARTNERSHIP

"See, I am sending my messenger ahead of you, who will prepare your way before you."(Matthew 11:10b)

Stories about John's ministry in the wilderness had spread far and wide. Many had traveled to see John, and many had confessed, repented of their sins, and received the gift of baptism. But many others considered John's ministry a spectacle. They did not know what to make of his activities.

Jesus asked them to consider these questions:

"What did you go out into the wilderness to look at? A reed shaken by the wind? What then did you go out to see? Someone dressed in soft robes? Look, those who wear soft robes are in royal palaces. What then did you go out to see? A prophet? Yes, I tell you, and more than a prophet."(Matthew 11:7b-9)

The authorities who had imprisoned John likely hoped that the winds of assault on John's character would ensure that his ministry collapsed. But Jesus confirmed otherwise: "This is the one about whom it is written, 'See, I am sending my messenger ahead of you, who will prepare your way before you'" (Matthew 11:10). John was not the Messiah, but God intended for John to work in partnership with Jesus.

Partnership is antithetical to jealously. Jealousy makes us think in a single-minded fashion and urges us to elevate our own accomplishments, our own agendas over others. Jealousy causes us to look out for our own self-interest. Jealousy drives us to covet the gifts of others—sometimes even to the point of trying to discredit them. Jealousy views partnership as a threat to individuality; the last thing jealousy wants is to share the limelight with others.

If you find yourself comparing yourself to others, noticing their achievements, and gauging your self-worth by what they are doing, look to Jesus and ask him to help you focus on God's accomplishments. If you find yourself looking to others to shape your life, ask Jesus to teach you how to use the unique gifts he has given you for the benefit of others.

Ask Jesus to help you be content in the roles, responsibilities, and skills he has given you. Then ask him to send others with whom you can partner in ministry to build bridges, restore communities, and look out for the welfare of others. Through Jesus' love, anything you accomplish will point to his authority.

PRAYER

Jesus, help me to fix my eyes on you. When I begin to turn my mind to jealous thoughts, help me to surrender those thoughts of ill will to you so I can be freed from the scourge of this emotion. Amen.

GOD'S VALUE SYSTEM

"Truly I tell you, among those born of women no one has arisen greater than John the Baptist."(Matthew 11:11a)

Jesus honored John by proclaiming that "no one has arisen greater." What a remarkable statement. After all, John lived a humble life in the desert, with no material possessions and no sign of anything his society might have deemed a "success."

Even in his mother's womb, John revered Jesus. When Mary was pregnant with Jesus, she visited her cousin Elizabeth, who was pregnant with John. When Mary greeted Elizabeth, John leaped in his mother's womb. Even as a fetus, John rejoiced being in the presence of the unborn Jesus (Luke 1:39-45).

As an adult, Jesus also showed much respect for John. Jesus could have been jealous of John's popularity. After all, John had baptized multitudes of people, and many wondered whether he was the Messiah. But Jesus never challenged John's ministry or felt the need to compete with him. Jesus even asked John to baptize him.

Jesus' affirming words of John were infused with appreciation, not envy. They resonated with God's love, putting Jesus' admiration and love for John at the forefront. Everything about Jesus was antithetical to jealousy. Jealousy tends to ignore the fullness of humanity by reducing people to a behavior or trait that aims to diminish their value and worth. But Jesus celebrates the full value of every person, seeing our flaws but seeing our potential as well, through the eyes of love.

Ask Jesus to help you honor others in the way Jesus honored John. Ask him to help you see every person through his eyes, as a unique creation, a gift from God, and to replace your jealous thoughts with love and a desire to reconcile and partner with others.

If you find this difficult to do, ask Jesus to help you celebrate and partner with those who are advancing his love and justice to a world in need of his healing touch. As you see the work Jesus is doing, thank him for the ways he is helping you to care for others. Rather than feeling jealous, you can rejoice in the transformation of lives, giving credit to Jesus and savoring his presence in your life.

PRAYER

Jesus, help me to honor others by valuing them for who you call them to be. Help me not to feel left out when another person receives recognition. Encourage me to see and celebrate the uniqueness of each person you have created. Amen.

PUTTING JEALOUSY INTO PERSPECTIVE

"The least in the kingdom of heaven is greater than he."(Matthew 11:11b)

No sooner had Jesus said, "No one has risen greater than John" he continued in the same breath to say, "The least in the kingdom of heaven is greater than he." This sounds like quite a contradiction.

Yet in God's kingdom, the least are actually given the title of "greater." Think of Jesus' teachings: "Blessed are the poor in spirit, for theirs is the kingdom of heaven" (Matthew 5:3); "Blessed are the meek, for they will inherit the earth" (Matthew 5:5); "Blessed are those who are persecuted for righteousness' sake, for theirs is the kingdom of heaven" (Matthew 5:10).

This perspective is central to Jesus' message of hope to the most disenfranchised members of society. He loves those whom society identifies as the least. For those who occupy the lowest rung of the social ladder, Jesus' words are a healing balm. He honors and respects them in a world that identifies them as "less than" worthy to be valued. And herein lies the key to being free of jealousy.

Oftentimes the root of jealousy is grounded in a preoccupation with other people's stations in life. You might covet someone's lifestyle and become bitter about the privileges they enjoy that you don't. You might get caught up in the comparison game, which breeds a sense of unease and a perpetual state of discontent. And when you find yourself engrossed with the reputation of others, you end up becoming dissatisfied with your life.

Turn your gaze back to Jesus. Focus on his words and purpose for his people, his mission to forgive, to heal, to love, to bring justice to the world. Jealousy cannot take root in your heart and dominate your thoughts if you ask Jesus to shape the mission of your life and help you to have compassion for those less fortunate than yourself. As you care for others, you will be humbled. In the process of serving others, you will learn from the people you serve. You will recognize your own need for Jesus' healing and love, and discover your own need to be cared for by others.

As you live by Jesus' teaching, your jealousies will be redirected to another perspective:

Clothe yourselves with compassion, kindness, humility, meekness, and patience . . . forgive each other; just as the LORD has forgiven you, so you also must forgive. Above all, clothe yourselves with love . . . Let the word of Christ dwell in you richly, teach and admonish one another in all wisdom. (Colossians 3:12b-16a)

PRAYER

Jesus, replace my thoughts of jealousy with thoughts of love, and help me to be transformed by your words so I can live out your mission for my life. Amen.

GLORIFY GOD

"If I glorify myself, my glory is nothing. It is my Father who glorifies me, he of whom you say, 'He is our God.'"(John 8:54)

Jealousy seeks attention for itself. It is suspicious of others. It does not look to God for guidance but strives to rule over others by any means necessary. Criticizing and destroying the reputation of others is a primary goal of jealousy. To be the center of attention is jealousy's aim, even as it stands in the background waiting to be noticed by others.

Throughout all the challenges Jesus confronted in his ministry, Jesus never sought to gain glory for himself. When the religious establishment tried to discredit his teaching, Jesus responded by saying, "Yet I do not seek my own glory; there is one who seeks it and he is the judge" (John 8:50).

A wonderful feature of the Bible is that it does not shy away from the complex nature of our human condition. Jesus recognizes jealousy as an insatiable desire to be seen, heard, praised, and noticed by others. He understands that we thirst for acceptance, significance, and relevance. Only one person can quench the thirst that drives jealousy. It is the one who says, "Let anyone who is thirsty come to me, and let the one who believes in me drink. As the scripture has said, 'Out of the believer's heart shall flow rivers of living water'" (John 7:37b-38).

If you find yourself discouraged when the spotlight does not shine on your accomplishments, if you find yourself craving acknowledgment and are willing to put others down to get it, bring your raw emotions to Jesus. Ask him to transform your jealous thoughts. Ask him to help you glorify God rather than yourself.

PRAYER

Jesus, help me to glorify you so I can be set free from my jealous thoughts. Help me to live by the liberating properties of your words. Amen.

MANAGING JEALOUSY

The following guidelines offer some ideas of how you can triumph over jealousy. Whatever strategies you decide to employ, allow Jesus to guide you in implementing them in your life. Permit Jesus to lead you into a lifestyle that allows you to be content in the knowledge and experience that Jesus is enough.

1. Tell Jesus about your feelings. Don't be ashamed to admit to yourself and to Jesus that you are harboring feelings of jealousy.

Biblical wisdom underscores God's understanding that you might crave another person's possessions or yearn to attain their lifestyle: "Neither shall you covet your neighbor's wife. Neither shall you desire your neighbor's house, or field, or male or female slave, or ox, or donkey, or anything that belongs to your neighbor" (Deuteronomy 5:21). Placing emphasis on what others have will leave you feeling restless. Desiring another person's belongings is a futile effort because nothing or no one can satisfy you or fulfill your needs like Jesus.

God also understands that coveting someone else's relationships will invite discontentment. Or you may be jealous of someone's youth and their ability to do things that you can no longer do or never had the opportunity to try. This kind of jealousy diverts your attention away from the gifts God has brought your way, away from what God has done and desires to do in your life.

You can tell Jesus whatever is on your mind. He won't ridicule you or dismiss your concerns. He won't take your emotional pains lightly. He wants to love you through your angst and transform you.

You might find it helpful to write your feelings of jealousy on a piece of paper and lift them up to Jesus as a symbolic gesture of submission to his wisdom. Or verbally offer your confession to Jesus, silently or aloud. Ask him to help you surrender to him those thoughts and desires that breed discontentment within you. Then ask Jesus to show you how he has blessed you.

These moments of sharing can become a time for you to draw closer to Jesus and experience deeper levels of his love.

Since, then, we have a great high priest who has passed through the heavens, Jesus, the Son of God, let us hold fast to our confession. For we do not have a high priest who is unable to sympathize with our weaknesses, but we have one who in every respect has been tested as we are, yet without sin. Let us therefore approach the throne of grace with boldness, so that we may receive mercy and find grace to help in time of need. (Hebrews 4:14-16)

2. Consider the damage jealousy can cause. *Jealousy invites turmoil. Your jealousy can affect more than one person.*

Jealousy has a tendency to nurture impulsive actions. Consider this statement from the Book of Proverbs: "For jealousy arouses a husband's fury, and he shows no restraint when he takes revenge" (Proverbs 6:34).

Jealousy can lead you to actions that leave Jesus out of the picture. Jealously does not welcome insights from God. At its core, jealousy reveals the areas of your life where you do not trust God. And before long, more than one person can become entwined in your net of jealousy.

Whatever feelings of jealousy rise within you, Jesus can release you from these thoughts. He can forgive you for behaviors that may be destructive or spiritually debilitating. Begin by asking Jesus to forgive you for the ways you have stored jealousy in your heart. Ask him for forgiveness if your actions have hurt another person or caused someone to mistreat others.

3. Remember who is the greatest. *When you focus on other people, when you become enamored with attaining the material things of this world, it is easy to forget that no one or thing is greater than Jesus.*

Jesus' love is unmatchable, his mercy everlasting, his power unlimited. His forgiveness will bring healing to your life. Ask Jesus to remind you of the magnificence of God as the Great Provider. As you acknowledge God's presence in the world, you can surrender those things that you prize so highly and be humbled in your Creator's presence.

For the one who is in you is greater than the one who is in the world. (1 John 4:4b)

4. Live in Jesus' love. *Learning to be content in Jesus means finding peace in the knowledge that his love, provision, and presence in your life can fulfill your needs.*

If you want to live in peace, you need to take an active role in uprooting jealousy from your life. Ponder the narratives surrounding Jesus' life and acquaint yourself with his teachings. Let Jesus help you identify the areas of your life that prevent you from living in the freedom of his love.

When thoughts of jealousy creep into your mind, ask Jesus to renew your mind by helping you love the person who is the object of your covetousness. One way of doing this is to imagine yourself as the person who is the object of your jealousy. Ask Jesus to reveal to you what he wants you to learn as you reflect on the role of jealousy in your life. Ask him to teach you how to love him with your whole heart, mind, body, and soul—and to love as he loves. If you are willing, Jesus can release you from your thoughts of envy and teach you how to love through the power of his love.

As you learn to surrender your life to his love, as you learn to abide in his love, you will love others not out of your imperfect love, but out of the fathomless love of Jesus (see John 15:7-11).

5. Find an accountability partner. *Allowing someone to pray for you and to hear, without judgment, your honest report of your progress can provide the partnership you need to help conquer your feelings of jealousy.*

When you are trying to overcome feelings of jealousy, an accountability partner can walk alongside you in your journey. They can ask you the hard questions and lovingly support you through your struggles. They can pray for you and tenderly inquire how you are dealing with the issue of jealousy in your life. Look for someone who will be quick to listen and slow to speak, someone who will not judge you but will also not pander to your feelings of jealousy. Find someone who will keep at the forefront the value of scripture, someone who will direct you not to themselves but to Jesus.

Ask Jesus to direct you to a trusted individual who can keep your confidence. This is important because you may be jealous of someone whom many people know. Or the source of your jealousy may entail a sensitive subject that should not be shared with everyone. Give Jesus time to

speak to your heart and ask him to give you peace about the person with whom you will share your intimate thoughts.

6. Seek help. *Sometimes jealous cravings can indicate that you are avoiding a difficult matter in your life.*

If you are sensing that your preoccupation with the lives of others may be a way of deflecting attention away from your own unresolved issues, seek the services of a counselor who can help you heal from your past and current pain. Couple this healing process with the partnership of others who will pray for you as you work toward achieving freedom from jealousy. And if you are not sure whether your feelings of jealousy are signs of avoiding your own problems, ask Jesus to reveal this to you.

For the commandment is a lamp and the teaching a light. (Proverbs 6:23a)

7. Practice contentment. *Learning to be content with being a child of God can free you from the scourge of jealousy.*

When Jesus said, "You cannot serve God and wealth" (Luke 16:13d), he understood that we can treat money and the things it can buy as our god; the allure of wealth and the trappings that come with it can enslave us.

Jesus does not reject or discriminate against wealthy people, but he does caution us that when we serve him, when we love him, we must love him with our whole heart, mind, body, and soul. He must be first in our lives; only then will we experience true wealth.

The treasure you can find in the love of Jesus is more valuable than anything on this earth, and it is everlasting. When the sentiments of jealousy invade your thoughts, ask Jesus to help you experience contentment as a beloved son or daughter of God.

You may need to allow Jesus to do a little pruning in your life. For a while, you may need to abstain from the things or situations that cause you to feel jealous of another person. You may need to avoid entering into conversations with those who fuel your desire to possess what others have. This may be painful at first. A kind of grieving may take place as you find yourself missing those things and people who have nurtured

your jealousy. Recognize this pain as an indication of how much you have rooted your self-worth in the love of things and people.

Like a weak muscle, your experience of contentment needs exercise to strengthen it. Spend some time each day taking notice of God's gifts. Ask Jesus to help you focus on his goodness and love for you. Remember that his love is not dependent on what you do for a living or what you own. He is more than able to provide for your needs (Matthew 6:31-33).

My prayer for you: I pray that you will allow Jesus to free you from the bondage of jealousy so you can live in the freedom of his love. For only in his love will you find true contentment, hope, and peace. Amen.

5. FEAR

As she ran down the street, she could not feel her feet pounding the concrete. When she reached her house, the only thing she could feel was the drum of her heart. After fumbling to insert her key into the lock, she flung open the front door, dropped her backpack onto the floor, tore into the hallway, and called out to her father. He rushed to the door, and when she caught sight of him, she buried her face into the soft pouch of his stomach.

"What's the matter?" he asked.

Tears lined her face as she tried to speak, but the halting pace of her breathing stilled the words in her throat. He laid his hand across the gap between her shoulder blades and guided her into the living room. When he reached his favorite armchair, he leaned against one of its worn-out arms, where the speckled coffee stains blotted the fabric print. He motioned her to stand still for a moment, while he eased himself down into the sagging seat. Gently, he hoisted her onto his lap, weaving his hand into hers and cradling her. She laid her head on his chest until her hurting cries eased into a whimper. Before long, she was ready to speak.

She told him that a girl at school had called her "retarded." To make matters worse, some of her friends stood by and said nothing in her defense. All day she had tried to pretend that it did not hurt, but the words resounded in her mind like a refrain.

As her father listened, he sensed that unspoken fears lay beneath the surface of her story. She may not have been conscious of these fears, she may not have been able to formulate words to describe the nature of these particular feelings, but he believed that she feared going back to school because she would be the butt of her schoolmates' jokes. With this unspoken fear came others. She feared that the children in her school would distance themselves from her, and most of all she feared she would no longer be popular.

After listening to his daughter's story, her father cupped her face in his hands and said, "Well, you know the child who said you are retarded is entitled to her opinion."

A puzzled frown crossed his daughter's face.

"The question is, do you think you are retarded?"

The girl silently shook her head.

Her father smiled. "My dear one, the girl who called you names was probably looking for attention. Maybe she wanted someone to notice her. Or maybe she just doesn't like you. There will always be people in life who dislike you for one reason or another. The important thing is not to let the opinions of someone else shape how you see yourself and what you believe about yourself."

She listened thoughtfully.

He continued. "Are you afraid of losing your friends because of what this person said about you?"

She nodded.

He replied "I thought so. You know, dear heart, the things people say about you may hurt, but you must never be afraid of what others think about you. Always remember the most important words for you to live by are that Jesus loves you. Hold onto that. And you know the wonderful thing about Jesus is that you can tell him all about your fears and he will understand. And you know what? He can even turn your fears into joy."

It is often the unexpected incidents in our life that expose our deepest fears. Take Jesus' disciples, for example. In the course of his ministry, they were his closest companions. They witnessed him feed a multitude with a few bread and fish. They marveled at his ability to heal the sick and the lame. They watched him cast out demons. They sat under his teaching and stood in awe of his wisdom. They observed him praying, worked alongside him, and talked to him about anything that was in their hearts.

If there was any group of people who had no cause for fear, it was the disciples. And yet, they experienced fear. When a sudden storm wrapped around their boat, they were terrified. When Jesus was being persecuted by an unruly mob, they ran away.

And yet, when they called out to Jesus, he always came to their rescue. Even when they failed to call out to him, he did not turn his back

on them. When they forgot his faithfulness to them, he never abandoned them. When their doubts and fears gripped them, Jesus was always there for them.

Jesus understands that we will experience fear. If he did not, he would not have spoken about fear in his teachings or tried to calm the anxiety of his followers.

What causes you the most fear? When you experience fear, do you call out to Jesus for help? Or have you grown frustrated with asking Jesus to help you? Are you afraid of admitting your weakness to Jesus? Are you afraid of Jesus?

Learning about the character of Jesus, reading scripture, pondering his teachings, and learning about how he comes to the aid of his people will foster your trust in what Jesus can do in your life. He will hear your prayers and save you from drowning in the sea of your fears.

As you relinquish your fears to Jesus, try to be patient with yourself if those fears resurface periodically. Remember, if it took a while to cultivate a lifestyle of fear, it may take time to be healed of your fears.

I pray that, in time, you, too, will be able to believe and say:

I sought the LORD, and he answered me,
and delivered me from all my fears. (Psalm 34:4)

Give yourself a few minutes to consider Jesus' own fears:

And going a little farther, he threw himself on the ground and prayed,
"My Father, if it is possible, let this cup pass from me,
yet not what I want but what you want."(Matthew 26:39)

Fear gathers around him like a dead weight when he asks his friends to stay awake, but only silence echoes in the night scarred with stars. Anxiety sweeps over him as his feet scrape the ground. Soon grief beats him to his knees. He brings his face down to an earth marred with the footsteps of his distress. And with each breath, dust masks his face with its grime. In this lonely place he prays, "My Father, if it is possible, let this cup pass from me; yet not what I want but what you want" (Matthew 26:39).

Silence meets him as fear accompanies him on his journey toward death. He stands up and returns to his disciples. Then he says to Peter, "So, could you not stay awake with me one hour?" (Matthew 26:40b). His question remains unanswered as sleep holds Peter and the other disciples. Jesus lets them rest in their weariness, turns around, and returns to the lonely location where he prays and cries out again, "My Father, if this cannot pass unless I drink it, your will be done" (Matthew 26:42b).

He follows his lone footprints back to his sleeping friends. He does not disturb them. Instead, he leaves, walks back to his place of prayer, and for a third time he pauses and prays the same prayer again. The stars spread their imprint onto the sky. God draws time onto the solitary silhouette standing in the night. And Jesus stays awake.

THE LORD IS WITH YOU

In the sixth month the angel Gabriel was sent by God to a town in Galilee called Nazareth, to a virgin engaged to a man whose name was Joseph, of the house of David. The virgin's name was Mary. And he came to her and said, "Greetings, favored one! The Lord is with you." But she was much perplexed by his words and pondered what sort of greeting this might be. The angel said to her, "Do not be afraid, Mary, for you have found favor with God." (Luke 1:26-30)

Mary must have been understandably perplexed and mystified by the angel's greeting. Why would God send an angel to her? She must have shown signs of being afraid because the angel Gabriel assured her that she need "not be afraid."

Mary could have allowed any number of fears to occupy her thoughts permanently, but she did not. Instead, she contemplated the angel Gabriel's words and was eventually able to hear the message that "the Lord is with you." And notice that Mary pondered the nature of the angel Gabriel's message and gave herself time to make sense of his greeting.

Like Mary's encounter with the angel, you may be in a situation where you do not fully comprehend what is happening to you. But you can take comfort in knowing that whatever plans Jesus has for your life, he will lovingly walk alongside you. He is willing to listen to your questions, address your puzzlement, and calm your fears, even as you take the first step to follow him. Follow Mary's example and don't allow your fears to rush you into making hasty decisions about your future.

What does God have in store for you? Only Jesus can tell you that, but one thing is clear from this particular passage: You do not need to be afraid because, whatever is ahead for you, God is with you.

PRAYER

Jesus, thank you that you are with me. Thank you that you do not want me to be afraid. Help me to be open to the plans you have for my life and teach me to ponder your words so I can experience a greater sense of your love and care. Amen.

NOTHING WILL BE IMPOSSIBLE WITH GOD

"And now, you will conceive in your womb and bear a son, and you will name him Jesus. He will be great, and will be called the Son of the Most High, and the Lord God will give to him the throne of his ancestor David. He will reign over the house of Jacob forever, and of his kingdom there will be no end." Mary said to the angel, "How can this be, since I am a virgin?" The angel said to her . . . "nothing will be impossible with God." (Luke 1:31-35a, 37)

If Mary had reason to be afraid before the angel Gabriel told her she would give birth to God's son, there was a multitude of things that could have terrified her after she heard the news: Her fiancé, Joseph, leaving her. People distancing themselves from her when they learned she had conceived a child out of wedlock. Family abandoning her. Friends deserting her. Having no place to live, no way of providing for a child. Raising a child by herself. Public humiliation, even stoning.

Yet she asked only one question: "How can this be, since I am a virgin?"

Mary may well have been standing face to face with a celestial angel, but that did not stop her from finding out more about God's plans for her. Mary's response is a study in faith. Through the simple words, "Here am I," she presented herself wholly to God. By describing herself as "the servant of the Lord," she claimed her central identity. With her conclusion, "Let it be with me according to your word," she surrendered her fears—and her life—to God (Luke 1:38).

While you may be saying, "I'm no Mary," consider what you can learn from her. For starters, you do not need to be afraid to ask questions of God. When you are faced with a particularly trying situation that you do not understand, and fearful thoughts are running through your mind, ask Jesus to help you trust him. Ask him to bring people into your life to help you discern what God is calling you to do.

Spend time with Jesus, praying and reflecting on scripture. Ask Jesus to give you the courage you need. If you are having a hard time believing that "nothing will be impossible with God," ask Jesus to help you believe this truth.

Give God your fears and let God perform the impossible in your life.

PRAYER

Jesus, thank you that I can come to you with my questions. Help me to trust that you will guide me through the unexpected and uneasy moments in my life when I don't understand what's ahead for me. Thank you that nothing is impossible with God. Amen.

THE POWER OF PRAISE

And Mary said,"My soul magnifies the Lord, and my spirit rejoices in God my Savior."(Luke 1:46-47)

Mary had a choice. She could have lived in fear of what was going to happen to her, but instead she chose joy. With a glorious refrain of praise, she worshiped God, celebrating that "the Mighty One has done great things for me" (Luke 1:49). She directed her complete attention on God, giving all of herself in joyful abandonment.

If you have ever been terrified of something, you know how fear can propel you into a state of emotional and spiritual trauma. Fear has a tendency to block out or dismiss all the good things God has done.

But praise is a powerful counterbalance. When you are filled with praise for God, there is no room for fear to take hold.

Take a closer look at Mary's "Magnificat" (Luke 1:46-55). It contains a valuable lesson for keeping fear from shaping your life choices. Mary's sole focus was on the character of God. She praised God as holy, merciful, strong, a champion of the lowly, a feeder of the hungry, a keeper of promises.

When Mary proclaimed that "his mercy is for those who fear him" (Luke 1:50), she was not advocating fear of God, but rather awe of God: marveling at what God has done, can do, and will do for your life.

Just as Mary believed that God would do great things for her, so you can claim the great things that God will do for you. Consider God's promises to protect and strengthen you, to lift you up and fill you with good things, to be strong when you are weak. Nothing or no one can match God's power. As the Psalmist proclaims, "Your power and your righteousness, O God, reach the high heavens" (Psalm 71:18d-19).

The next time you experience fear, ponder God's abilities as the Creator of all things. Ask Jesus to remind you of God's promise, "'I will never leave you or forsake you.' So [you] can say with confidence, 'The LORD is my helper; I will not be afraid. What can anyone do to me?'" (Hebrews 13:5b-6).

PRAYER

Jesus, help me to praise you even in my fear, for in the calm of your protection, fear has no home. As I seek shelter in your refuge, teach me to adore your name. Teach me that the power of praise can lift me from the mire of my thoughts to a place of peace that can only be found in you. Amen.

DO NOT BE DISCOURAGED

Immediately he made the disciples get into the boat and go on ahead to the other side, while he dismissed the crowds. And after he had dismissed the crowds, he went up the mountain by himself to pray. When evening came, he was there alone, but by this time the boat, battered by the waves, was far from the land, for the wind was against them. (Matthew 14:22-24)

Jesus had just fed five thousand people by multiplying five loaves and two fish when he instructed his disciples to take a boat and go on ahead to Bethsaida. He was going to retreat to a mountain to pray.

As day drifted into evening, all appeared to be calm. But as Jesus was praying, turbulent winds suddenly came up on the sea, whipping around the disciples' boat. As experienced fishermen, the disciples were probably no strangers to unexpected storms. We can imagine their struggle to maneuver their boat against the howling wind. Perhaps as the storm strengthened, as waves threatened to engulf their craft, they had trouble maintaining control. Panic might easily have taken hold.

Did they shout at one another over the wind, working as a team to save their vessel—and their lives? Did they even think to cry out to Jesus? Maybe they blamed Jesus for sending them out in the boat in the first place.

There may be times in your life when sudden turbulence threatens to overwhelm you. The survival skills that have gotten you through tough times in the past might be taxed to the limit. You may feel as if all your know-how and experience are not going to get you through this storm.

It is during these times of vulnerability that you can recognize on a deeper level your need for help. However, like the disciples, asking Jesus for help may be the last thought that comes to mind when you are wrestling with fear, when all you can feel is the storm's relentless onslaught.

When you are in a difficult episode, do not be hard on yourself if you fail to recall Jesus' teachings: "My sheep hear my voice. I know them, and they follow me. I give them eternal life, and they will never perish. No one will snatch them out of my hand" (John 10:27-28).

Do not be discouraged if you forget the biblical words of wisdom, assuring you that during times of adversity, "The LORD is near to all who call on him" (Psalm 145:18a).

Instead, be encouraged that Jesus knows you can sometimes forget his promise that he will always be with you. He understands that you may feel alone. But he is always there, and he will never leave or forsake you.

PRAYER

Jesus, thank you for hearing my cries. Thank you for your promise to care for and protect me, even when I find myself forgetting. Amen.

THE SAME YESTERDAY, TODAY, AND FOREVER

And early in the morning he came walking toward them on the sea.
(Matthew 14:25)

From his mountain solitude and sanctuary of prayer, Jesus witnessed his disciples' attempt to regain control of their boat. As dawn gave birth to morning, he set out to meet his disciples in their time of need. He responded to their cries and had compassion on them.

Take heart from this. Even when you do not believe that Jesus is nearby, he is always close at hand, ready to respond to your request for assistance. Just as Jesus did not abandon the disciples, so he will not desert you or ignore your pleas for help. He will bring you through your fear.

Think about the disciples' situation. They had been in the boat for most of the evening before the storm hit. They had not been afraid when the seas were calm, and they had felt no need to cry out to Jesus. Had they allowed the tranquil surroundings to give them a false sense of security? Likewise, when things are relatively quiet in your life, do you recognize your need for Jesus? Then, when your fear arises, do you waver in your belief that Jesus can carry you through?

Fear has a tenacious tendency to breed more fear. If you cannot sense Jesus' presence, you may grow even more afraid. Your fear can cause you to forget the times Jesus has helped you in the past.

The lesson in this story is that, though the situation changes, "Jesus Christ is the same yesterday and today and forever" (Hebrews 13:8). He will be with you when the seas of your life are calm, and he will not avoid your storms. He will step right into the tempest to save you. His power and wisdom can overcome any circumstance you face.

So whether you are in or out of a stormy life experience, ask Jesus to help you sense his presence and believe his words that he will be with you. No erratic squall can sway the love, power, and protection of Jesus.

PRAYER

Jesus, when fear threatens to immerse me in hopelessness, help me to be in touch with your presence. Thank you that your love will always come to my rescue. Thank you that you will never let me battle my fears alone. Jesus, help me to see and hear and feel that you are "the same yesterday, today, and forever." Amen.

"DO NOT BE AFRAID"

But when the disciples saw him walking on the sea, they were terrified, saying,
"It is a ghost!" And they cried out in fear. But immediately Jesus spoke to them
and said, "Take heart, it is I; do not be afraid." (Matthew 14:26-27)

The disciples had spent many days and hours with Jesus. They witnessed him perform many miraculous deeds. They experienced his help when they were in need. And yet, when confronted with a frightening situation, they forgot everything.

When they saw a shadowy form approaching them across the water, they thought at first it was a ghost. This only ignited their panic further. None of the twelve recognized Jesus.

Jesus' first words to them were "Take heart." He did not ridicule or judge them for not realizing that it was indeed he. He never dismissed their fears.

Only after addressing their emotional state did Jesus identify himself by proclaiming, "It is I." His words of assurance reached out to them as if he were taking a crying child into his arms. And like a parent consoling his beloved children, he tenderly reassured them that they would be just fine.

Jesus' love is not dependent on, or influenced by, how we react to the trials of life. When you are afraid, when the storm surrounding you seems like more than you can withstand, when you do not recognize Jesus' presence, he reaches out to you with his tender words, "Take heart." Let his words, "Do not be afraid," bring you a deep peace that only his unconditional love can offer.

PRAYER

Jesus, teach me to live in the peace that can be mine when I receive your words of
comfort, guidance, and love. Amen.

A STEP OF FAITH

Peter answered him, "Lord, if it is you, command me to come to you on the water." He said, "Come." (Matthew 14:28-29a)

While the fears of the other men in the boat appeared to have been calmed by the words of Jesus, one of the disciples needed further proof that this person walking toward them was indeed who he claimed to be. Peter challenged Jesus, saying, "Lord, if it is you, command me to come to you on the water."

Jesus did not respond with harsh words, nor did he admonish Peter for his unbelief. He simply said, "Come." And in the fabric of this word, his invitation is clear. Even while the storm still rages, even when our doubts and fears are greatest, Jesus invites us to step out of the boat and come to him.

Maybe you read the Bible, go to church, and attend Bible studies, but suddenly you find yourself in a terrifying situation. You wonder whether Jesus will come through for you. You might be able to recall instances when Jesus helped you during a past time of crisis, but you find yourself questioning if he can help this time. Maybe your doubts feel as big as the waves that threaten to swamp your life.

Just as Jesus did not dismiss Peter's need for assurance, so he will not ignore your pleas for more clarification or proof of his existence. The question is, are you prepared to come to him when he calls? Are you prepared to follow Peter's example and step out of the place where you are most fearful and trust Jesus' guidance?

PRAYER

Jesus, help me to have the courage to call out to you when I am afraid. And help me to follow your instructions on how I can combat my fears. Amen.

HEAR MY CRY

So Peter got out of the boat, started walking on the water, and came toward Jesus. But when he noticed the strong wind, he became frightened, and beginning to sink, he cried out, "Lord, save me!" (Matthew 14:29b-30)

When Jesus uttered the word, "Come," Peter stepped out of the boat without hesitation. As Peter trod the waters, it was as if the moving sea had formed a second skin under his feet. Right ahead of him stood Jesus, and it was on Jesus that Peter focused all his attention.

When he looked to Jesus, he walked with direction and purpose. He was fearless. When he looked at Jesus, courage surfaced within him. He was bold. As he moved toward Jesus, the storm did not seem to faze him. He was not afraid.

But once he turned his attention back to the menacing strength of the wind, fear gripped him. Peter began to sink. Feeling as if the waters would swallow him whole, he cried out, "Lord, save me!"

Have you ever been in a place where troubles were swirling around you, and you started walking toward Jesus with what you considered a strong faith? But then other things or other people got in the way, and you lost your focus on him.

What about now? Do the trials you are facing at this time in your life threaten to overcome you and cause you to lose your grounding in Jesus? How long will you wait before you call out to him for help?

Jesus calls you to walk on the waters of faith. When anxiety and fear begin to take up residence in your heart, Jesus will always hear your cry—at the first sign of trouble or when you feel completely overwhelmed by fear.

PRAYER

Jesus, thank you that the rough seas of my troubles will never overpower you. Thank you that even when I lose my way, even when I fail to look at you and I let fear breed within me, you are there to hear my cry. Amen.

REFOCUS

Jesus immediately reached out his hand and caught him, saying to him, "You of little faith, why did you doubt?" When they got into the boat, the wind ceased. And those in the boat worshiped him, saying, "Truly you are the Son of God." (Matthew 14:31-33)

Jesus' response to Peter's fear was immediate. He reached out his hand and caught Peter. As Jesus took hold of him, he said, "You of little faith, why did you doubt?" Peter did not respond to Jesus' question; neither did Jesus try to answer this question for him. Instead, the question was left for Peter to ponder.

Choosing not to chastise Peter for having so little faith, Jesus stepped into the boat, and the wind's unruly force came to a complete halt. Jesus had broken down the barriers of wind and waves, fear and doubt, and the disciples were finally ready to proclaim, "Truly you are the Son of God."

Where does your faith stand? With the doubts of Peter, with the worship of the disciples, or somewhere in between?

Know this: You may be prone to doubting Jesus when a rush of circumstances throws you into a sea of fear, but Jesus will always be a consistent, steadying presence in your life. No one or thing can overwhelm him.

When you lose sight of where you are headed, when you lose contact with Jesus, when your fears seem too big for you, keep your eyes focused on him. Jesus will reach out to you even as you doubt his ability to save you. He will temper the storm even as you have no answers. He will step into the boat of your fears and help you refocus on his strength and love.

PRAYER

Jesus, help me to praise you in and out of my times of fear. Help me keep my focus on you and to trust you in all aspects of my life. Amen.

NEVER ALONE

Then Jesus went with them to a place called Gethsemane; and he said to his disciples, "Sit here while I go over there and pray." He took with him Peter and the two sons of Zebedee, and began to be grieved and agitated. Then he said to them, "I am deeply grieved, even to death; remain here, and stay awake with me." And going a little farther, he threw himself on the ground and prayed, "My Father, if it is possible, let this cup pass from me; yet not what I want but what you want." (Matthew 26:36-39)

As the time of Jesus' death approached, he expressed a vulnerability he had never shown his disciples before: He did not want to be alone. So he asked Peter, James, and John to accompany him to the place where he would pray. Eventually, he shared with them the depth of his feelings: "I am deeply grieved, even to death." In his humanity, Jesus experienced the loneliness, fear, and anguish that comes when we face death.

Though he clearly valued the presence of those around him, he never dismissed the One who would always be with him. Through it all, Jesus continued to pray. In agonizing words, Jesus laid bare his emotions before God.

Jesus' actions provide a model for us when we face our fears. His request that a few disciples stay with him tells us the importance of sharing in each other's burdens. His selection of three close disciples to partner him in this intimate part of his faith life reminds us to exercise discretion when we select those who will partner with us in our difficult hours. Jesus' reliance on prayer to get him through that arduous night models for us the importance of praying through all seasons of our lives, even when it is painful, even when we find it hard to understand all the feelings we are experiencing.

What is your first response in the face of fear? Do you reach out for help or do you close yourself off from others? Sometimes the hardest thing to do is to admit fear to others; you may find it easier to shield others from your needs. Or you may move in the opposite direction, becoming so dependent on others that you become less dependent on Jesus.

One thing you can be sure of: No matter what you face, no matter how alone you feel, Jesus will always stand by your side. You can honestly tell him what is going on in your heart, and he will hear your cry. Ask him to help you find people who will be there for you, to share in your struggle. Remember that Jesus modeled partnership; he does not intend for you to be alone.

PRAYER

Jesus, help me to reach out to you when I am struggling with fear. Help me to choose people who can accompany me through trying seasons in my life. Amen.

THE FRIEND WHO WON'T FAIL

Then he came to the disciples and found them sleeping; and he said to Peter, "So, could you not stay awake with me one hour? Stay awake and pray that you may not come into the time of trial; the spirit indeed is willing, but the flesh is weak." (Matthew 26:40-41)

When Jesus returned from his prayer, he found the very people he had counted on sound asleep. They were simply too weary to comply with his request to be with him. In his anguish Jesus asked, "So, could you not stay awake with me one hour? Stay awake and pray that you may not come into the time of trial."

Jesus' words reflected his concern that the disciples not be overwhelmed by the ensuing events they would soon face and yet, at the same time, he did not hide his disappointment that they could not stay awake with him——even one hour.

His words also reveal his understanding of human nature: "the spirit is willing, but the flesh is weak." Jesus knew that his disciples wanted to comply with his request; he understood that they did not intend to abandon him in his hour of need. But he also knew that, no matter how much they wanted to support him, they did not have the stamina to act upon their intentions.

There may be times in your life when, even though you have asked for support, someone will let you down. Perhaps someone who has been supportive of you in the past will not meet your expectations. Maybe a best friend will not have time to be with you because they are going through some hard times. Even if you understand their reasons, you may feel sad and disappointed. You may latch onto the fear of abandonment.

Allow your feelings to draw you closer to Jesus; share your sadness with him. Others may fail you, but Jesus will never leave you alone in your fears. By his power and love, he will help you overcome your distress. Share with him the underlying concerns that give rise to fear in your life. And then give him the time and the room to minister to you and teach you how you can live a life that is not ruled by fear.

PRAYER

Jesus, sometimes I struggle with accepting that people cannot be there for me in the way that I would like. Help me to understand and forgive those who are not able to stand by me in my time of need. Release me from the fear of abandonment, meet me at my point of loneliness, and help me to trust your promise that you will never leave me. Amen.

LEARNING TO OVERCOME FEAR

The following guidelines offer some ideas of how you can overcome your fears. Whatever strategies you decide to employ, allow Jesus to guide you in implementing them into your life. Find solace in Jesus' teachings and let him lead you into a lifestyle abounding in peace and filled with hope.

1. Surrender your fears to Jesus. *Jesus does not want you to deny your fears. He understands that you will struggle with this emotion, and he encourages you to share your concerns with him.*

Fears have a habit of multiplying. The more you think about your fears, the more they can become an intense presence in your thoughts. So when your fears surface, do not permit them to overpower you, but instead surrender them to Jesus and ask him to replace those fears with his peace.

Imagine sitting down and having a conversation with Jesus as if you were talking to a friend. Picture Jesus listening to you and not interrupting. When you have finished sharing your concerns with Jesus, hear him tenderly tell you that he will not let you confront these fears by yourself and that he will help you to overcome them.

Another way to give your fears to Jesus is to write a list of your fears on a piece of paper and place them at the foot of a cross, or hold them in the palm of your hand and lift them to Jesus as a sign of surrender. Whatever way you choose to share your fears with Jesus, he will respond to your heart cry.

Fear also has a habit of fixating on a single outcome of a situation and that scenario is often a pessimistic one or one that paints a hopeless picture. Fear does not see other available options, but Jesus does. When you turn to Jesus for guidance, he will always enable you to see beyond your fears, find hope in the present, and witness a brighter future.

Be prepared to come to Jesus each time a fearful thought or episode surfaces. Rather than seeing this as a burdensome process, look at it from a different perspective: Each time you come to Jesus and tell him about your fears, you can rejoice in the knowledge that, no matter how many times you approach him with your troubles, he will never grow weary of

your concerns. And when you pray to him, you will know that you are not alone.

If you feel the presence of fear even after you have surrendered your concerns to Jesus, do not be discouraged. Treat this as one more opportunity for Jesus to show you that he will never tire of your emotional struggles. And all the while, as you surrender your fears to Jesus, Jesus will be reminding you that he loves you and will not leave you or forsake you: "There is no fear in love, but perfect love casts out fear" (1 John 4:18a).

2. Ask Jesus to remind you of how he has addressed your fears in the past. *It is useful to recall Jesus' faithfulness to others and yourself as you confront a present fear.*

Fear has a propensity to block out the times when Jesus has faithfully enabled you to overcome your past troubles. Taking time to allow Jesus to help you recall those times when he has come to your aid can be a useful strategy in combating your current fears.

Pondering scripture is particularly helpful because God's words can remind you of God's faithfulness. They can also reinforce in your heart and mind that God is more than able to deal with your troubles and ease your fears:

> *When you pass through the waters, I will be with you; and through the rivers, they shall not overwhelm you; and when you walk through fire you shall not be burned, and the flame shall not consume you. For I am the LORD your God. (Isaiah 43:2-3a)*

As you read about Jesus' abilities to calm the fears of his disciples and followers, you can feel confident that he will do the same for you. Think again of the story of Jesus calming the wind while the disciples were in the boat. When the storm hit, their first inclination was not to cry out to Jesus for help. It was as if Jesus were out of sight and out of mind. Fear overtook their faculties as quickly as the storm swamped their vessel.

When Jesus appeared to them, he calmed the storm—and their fears. But they could have received his calming presence *before* actually seeing his

physical presence. If they had remembered his faithfulness to them in the past and recounted his teachings; if they had recalled the many miracles they had seen him perform; if they had drawn strength from his promises to them that he was their protector, they may well have triumphed over their fears a lot sooner. Indeed, they may well have prevented fear from grabbing onto their hearts.

Just as Jesus' faithfulness saved them from drowning in their fears, so too, when fear begins to brew in your mind and threaten to engulf you, ask Jesus to help you sense his presence. Even when you have little to no faith, even when you have doubts, Jesus' love will always rescue you. All you have to do is call out his name.

3. Offer worship and praise. *The last thing you may want to do when fear seizes you is to worship and praise God.*

If you are in the midst of a trial, you may feel frustrated with Jesus because your fears are not subsiding fast enough. You may not feel like praising God at all. You might think your worship is insincere. Whatever your feelings, ask Jesus to help you glorify God.

As you praise God, your fears will grow smaller and more manageable because you will have immersed yourself in the strength of God. Praise is a great reminder of the Creator's unmatchable value and worth, whose faithfulness is never ending.

There are many ways and reasons to praise God. You can loudly praise God because he is "a rock of refuge" and "a strong fortress to save [you]" from your fears (Psalm 31:2b). You can utter words of praise to God in silence because he has promised that he will rescue you from the hand of your enemies (Psalm 31:15, 138:7-8). You can enter into a dance of praise to God because God's love will turn your "mourning into dancing" (Psalm 30:11). You may find it easier to sit down, close your eyes, and sing some hymns or gospel songs that you know from memory, while thanking God for forgiving your sins and transgressions (Psalm 32). You may kneel, or bow down or lie prostrate. Whatever position of reverence you choose, you can worship God because "at a time of distress, the rush of mighty waters shall not reach [you]" because God is your "hiding place" and God will "preserve [you] from trouble" and "surround [you] with glad cries of deliverance" (Psalm 32:6b-7).

Set aside a moment of your day for praise. At first you might only be able to dedicate a few minutes a day to this discipline. Whatever amount of time you set aside to lifting up God's name in praise, your openness to enter into this activity embodies God's wisdom that he has not given you a spirit of fear, "but rather a spirit of power and of love and self-discipline" (2 Timothy 1:7b).

When you praise God, you access the spirit of power and of love that is available to you. By exercising self-discipline in building a lifestyle of praise, you are rejecting fear in favor of depending on God's ability to get you through the storms of life. Do not let fear win the day. Walk in the freeing attributes of praise, and be awakened to the blessings God wants to bestow upon you.

4. Get away to pray. *To follow Jesus' example of going to a quiet place to be in prayer is a step toward replacing your fears with God's assurance that he is with you.*

When Jesus was afraid, he went to the Garden of Gethsemane and shared his anguish in prayer with God. There may well be times when you will have to journey to a place where you can get away from your daily commitments. Like Jesus, you can honestly tell God about your fears and listen for God's reassurance that he will strengthen you for the trials you are confronting.

Notice that, though Jesus struggled with emotional pain, he did not leave his disciples altogether. In fact, he was in prayer for them, and by so doing, he rose above the tendency of fear that causes us to turn our back's on other peoples' needs.

5. Ask others to pray for you. *You do not have to confront your fears alone.*

When you are facing a fearful situation, ask Jesus to lead you to people who will pray for you and be a support network for you. God hears the prayers of his people and is always willing to respond to the heart cries of his children:

> *Again, truly I tell you, if two of you agree on earth about anything you ask, it will be done for you by my Father in heaven. For where two or three are gathered in my name, I am there among them. (Matthew 18:19-20)*

You may find it difficult to ask people to pray for you. Perhaps you are in a position of leadership and do not want others to know of your weaknesses. Perhaps you have been told that you are a failure if you share your shortcomings and struggles with others. But when you ask others to pray for you, a community of support and fellowship awaits you.

You might find it a relief to know that you are not the only one who struggles with fears. You will also find comfort in the knowledge that you do not have to be in denial about your emotions and that you do not have to be superhuman. Asking people to pray for you also reminds you that you are not alone. Not only is Jesus with you, not only does Jesus hear your cries, but Jesus will provide you with the partnership of others to help you get through the difficult seasons of your life. Ask Jesus to direct you to those with whom you can share your fears in confidence. Sometimes your fears can weaken you spiritually to the point that you are too worn out even to pray. The prayers of a people can shore up your spirit and lift you up to a God who will never let you fall into the abyss of your fears.

6. Be persistent. *Do not be surprised if ideas, pictures, sounds, and smells that remind you of your fears resurface. Take courage. Do not lose heart. Jesus will help you combat these fears.*

There are times when you may find that your fears persist. Remember the Apostle Paul's warning that "our struggle is not against enemies of blood and flesh, but against the rulers, against the authorities, against the cosmic powers of this present darkness, against the spiritual forces of evil in the heavenly places" (Ephesians 6:12).

Paul's words are a clear indicator that you need to place any struggles you have into context by taking into account that there can be other forces at play. The devil can prey on your fears and cause you to forget God's faithfulness. Before long, your fears can dominate your thoughts. When you think you can't absorb any more fear, more fears can resurface and breed discouragement and eventually a sense of hopelessness.

While acknowledging the presence of these spiritual evil forces, Paul presents a strategy on how to fight and triumph spiritually over the devil's conniving ploys. His advice is to "take up the whole armor of God, so that

you may be able to withstand on that evil day, and having done everything, to stand firm" (Ephesians 6:13).

But you may ask, what does it really mean to put on "the armor of God"? How can I do this? One way is to personalize your reading of scripture by replacing the pronouns "you" or "we" with "I" or "my." Such an insertion can help make the Bible more relevant to your life. And you can imagine yourself putting on these spiritual garments of victory and standing triumphantly in the face of all you confront:

> I will stand therefore, and fasten the belt of truth around my waist, and put on the breastplate of righteousness. As shoes for my feet I will put on whatever will make me ready to proclaim the gospel of peace. With all these, I will take the shield of faith, with which I will be able to quench all the flaming arrows of the evil one. (Ephesians 6:14-16)

No matter how many times your fears pop up during the day, you can arm yourself with scripture that speaks to Jesus' goodness and awesome power: "Finally, be strong in the Lord and in the strength of his power" (Ephesians 6:10).

Stop and let this sink in. You don't have to be strong in your own strength. It is God's power that will guide you. When you equip yourself with God's spiritual armor, there is not one part of your life that God cannot protect.

7. Call on the name of Jesus. *You can call on Jesus, and he will rescue you from your fears.*

When Peter and John healed a crippled beggar, they did so in the authority of Jesus' name (Acts 3:1-10). In an attempt to explain to the crowd the factors that contributed to this man's healing, Peter announced, "And by faith in his name, his name itself has made this man strong, whom you see and know; and the faith that is through Jesus has given him this perfect health in the presence of all of you" (Acts 3:16).

The utterance of Jesus' name is enough to save you from fear. In Jesus' name you can speak the words of scripture silently or aloud. There is no situation that Jesus cannot transform. So when fear arises, you do

not need to be entrapped by its clutches. Instead, call on the name of Jesus and ask for his hope, peace, and love to reside in your mind, body, and soul. By his name, God's perfect love will banish fear from your thoughts.

There is no fear, but perfect love casts out fear. (1 John 4:18a)

My prayer for you: I pray that Jesus' teachings and life will show you how he can assist you through emotional storms of fear. May your reflections on his life and ministry help you to trust his promise of protection and care. I pray that you will receive Jesus' words of comfort, guidance, and love. Amen.

6. ANGER

When he first told me, my words of initial disbelief retreated into silence. It was an all-too-familiar story of a teacher abusing authority, and it still managed to surprise and disgust me. My friend revealed that his instructor had just dismissed him permanently from her class. When he told me the instructor's reasons, I was infuriated. He had approached her to discuss some of his concerns about how the course was being conducted. Frustrated by the poor quality of teaching he was receiving, my friend gingerly raised the issue of her poor class preparation and sketchy attendance. Not wanting to dismiss her abilities as a teacher, he asked for her assistance with his studies. Despite her uneven performance as an instructor, he believed he needed her expertise to successfully pass his exam. To minimize potential backlash, he exercised discretion and did not mention to her that he, like other students, also took issue with her unethical methods of using them to collect data for her doctoral research.

It had not been an easy decision for him to confront her, but his desire to learn and better his career options roused him to action, although reluctantly. Now this instructor was refusing him entry into her class, forcing him to pay a fee if he wanted to take his exams.

During my friend's sharing, I was struck by his calm demeanor. Even though he could have cleaved to his right to be angry, I could not detect a trace of hostility or bitterness in his voice. But he did express that he felt at a loss about how to proceed. I, on the other hand, was outraged. My friend was, and is, a decent, thoughtful young man who is smart and loves to learn. I could not stand to see academic support withheld from such a bright student. My anger gained momentum when I considered how this instructor would continue to squelch other students' academic potential. There seemed to be no recourse, no accountability, no consequences attached to this teacher's actions, and that enraged me.

I do not experience anger often, but over the years I have found that my anger is provoked when I am with people who share similar indignations about injustice. Granted, this circle of like-minded individuals can provide

me with emotional support, but I have to be careful not to align myself so much to this gathering of empathy that I fail to look to Jesus for guidance on how to respond effectively to injustices. Otherwise, it would be all too easy to turn my back on forging bridges of reconciliation. Sometimes my anger propels me to action. Sometimes my anger births a sense of hopelessness within me. I also have to be mindful not to allow my anger to evolve into a strong dislike of those who are the perpetrators of wrongdoing. I have discovered that when I cling to my belief with righteous indignation—especially when an issue of justice is at stake—I am dissuaded from appreciating the complex humanity of another person.

At one time in my life, it never would have dawned on me to tell Jesus about my anger or ask him how I could respond to a situation that infuriated me. Thankfully, a dear mentor advised me that, while she supported my impassioned feelings about injustice, she also knew that if I did not take charge of my anger, it could overwhelm me. This wise counsel led me on a journey of learning how to share my anger with Jesus and refocus my emotion into practical action.

In the process of my many conversations with Jesus, I have been touched by his understanding, comforted by his compassion, and relieved that he is not afraid or put off by my anger. These exchanges encourage me to be open to Jesus' wisdom as I rely on him to teach me how to manage my anger and deal with the issue at hand in a way that glorifies God. When my anger begins to instill doubt about Jesus' ability to address matters of concern to me—especially injustices that seem to go unpunished—I am learning to trust these issues to Jesus, even when they do not get resolved in the way that I would like. But this, too, is a process.

What are the triggers that can propel you into a state of rage? When you experience anger, do you communicate it in an overt or a passive manner? Or do you tend to ignore or suppress your anger because you are afraid of this emotion? Have you been told, indirectly or directly, that it is not good to express anger?

Scripture does not downplay the existence of anger. Think of the time Jesus "drove out all who were buying and selling in the temple" (Matthew 21:12). While neither the Apostle John or Matthew used the word "angry" to describe Jesus, his actions certainly convey that he was

not pleased with the way the merchants and buyers treated the temple as a marketplace, its holiness desecrated.

In another incident involving anger, one of the disciples let loose his rage when an unruly crowd came to arrest Jesus. Caught in the middle of this struggle, this disciple cut off the ear of a chief priest's slave. Jesus was quick to reprimand him for his actions before healing the man's ear (Luke 22:50-53). Another time, a throng threatened to throw stones at a woman who was accused of committing adultery. Jesus told them to consider their own propensity to sin before judging the victim and stoning her (John 8:3-11).

These scriptures can encourage us because they recognize anger as a universal emotion. We can and will experience anger in our lives. We do not have to live in denial and downplay or dismiss our angry thoughts. We do not have to feel guilty or ashamed about our anger. Sometimes it is a reaction to how a group of people has been mistreated. Such anger can energize us to follow Jesus' example by serving the needs of the poor and marginalized.

But there is a downside to anger. Other times anger may permeate our being, and we are not sure what spurs it. In these instances anger can be so destructive that it can blind us to the consequences of our actions and instill anger in others. If we do not seek Jesus' wisdom on how to manage our anger, when we cannot find a way to cope with it, we can harm ourselves by engaging in self-destructive behavior—or make others the objects of our anger. As a result, this emotion can distort our view of the world and hurt our relationships.

The challenge for all of us is not to deny this emotion but to take ownership of how our anger affects us and those around us, and to ask Jesus to help us find constructive ways to channel our anger. The question is, to what extent are we prepared to share the depths of our anger with Jesus?

When Jesus was angry, he did not allow his feelings to stop him from serving others; his care for the emotional and physical needs of others did not wane. He healed those who came to the temple in need of his touch. And he would have forgiven the money changers and merchants if they had come back asking for his forgiveness. Jesus understood there is a place for anger and the need for love, and he can help us find ways to address the things that make us angry.

Give yourself a few minutes to picture this scene of Jesus' anger:

Then Jesus entered the temple and drove out all who were selling and buying in the temple, and he overturned the tables of the money changers and the seats of those who sold doves. . . . The blind and the lame came to him in the temple, and he cured them. (Matthew 21:12,14)

The cattle shuffle in their cramped quarters, while nearby sheep bleat their calls in grating harmonies. Adding to the din, doves flap their wings against the bars of their cages. Their cooing rises and falls like the jangled sounds coming from a piano played by a child randomly hammering the keys.

Amplifying the cacophony are sellers yelling about the virtues of their wares. The clatter of money on the tables sounds like crabs scampering into the sea. Some in the temple courtyard are aggressive, shoving their goods into the faces of prospective buyers.

In the midst of this commotion, Jesus enters the temple and commands all who are selling and buying to leave the premises. One after another, Jesus grabs hold of the tables and seats used by the moneychangers to conduct their business and pushes them to the ground. An uproar ensues as coins spill over the floor, and the merchants scramble to recover their money.

Jesus does not appear to notice their agitation. He only continues to overturn more tables and seats. In anger, in anguish, he cries out, "It is written, 'My house shall be called a house of prayer'; but you are making it a den of robbers" (Matthew 21:13).

With these words, the money merchants scuttle away in shame before the blind and the lame come in droves.

And Jesus cures them.

TAKE CONTROL

Then Jesus entered the temple and drove out all who were selling and buying in the temple, and he overturned the tables of the money changers and the seats of those who sold doves. (Matthew 21:12)

Interestingly, it was the physical objects used to sell the merchants' wares—not the actual merchants—that Jesus pushed to the ground. This is in keeping with Jesus' character, because throughout the Gospel narratives no mention is ever made of Jesus physically harming anyone. Even when he was brutally persecuted, he never retaliated by inflicting violence on his enemies. Even though he was dismayed—perhaps even infuriated—by the desecration and dishonor he saw in the temple, he had control over his emotions.

It is also important to note that Jesus did not invite anyone to join him in his outburst. He did not need to surround himself with people who would foster his point of view or legitimate his cause. That might have quickly inflamed the situation out of control.

Anger is a very powerful emotion that can quickly take over. The goal is not to deny it but to manage it. The aim is not to fuel it but to understand it.

When you feel anger rising within you, call on Jesus' wisdom. Ask him to guide you, to show you how you can respond to the matter at hand. Ask him to teach you how to control your anger and make use of it in appropriate ways.

PRAYER

Jesus, help me to give to you my raw emotions. Thank you that I can turn my anger over to you. Amen.

RIGHTEOUS ANGER

He said to them, "It is written, 'My house shall be called a house of prayer'; but you are making it a den of robbers." (Matthew 21:13)

Jesus was clearly alarmed at the level of commerce going on in the temple, this holy place where prayer should have taken center stage. Traders, merchants, and money changers pursued their self-interests to further their own gain. They had made the temple into a "den of robbers." Perhaps some merchants were engaged in lawful trade, but the hustle and bustle of the market hardly created an atmosphere where people could seek God and quiet through the solace of prayer.

Note that Jesus' anger did not stifle his ability to express the reason for his anger. His frustration emerged from his righteous outrage that God's house, and God's intentions for this temple, were being ignored. The merchants had disregarded the primary purpose of the temple as "a house of prayer."

Have you ever experienced this kind of righteous anger? Maybe you are uncomfortable with the way something is being handled at your church. Perhaps you are angry about the poverty you see, an injustice in your community, or prejudice at work or school.

Communicating to Jesus through prayer can transform your anger into action guided by love. Ask Jesus to reveal to you how to respond to this biblical passage. Ask him to help you reflect God's desire to care for the poor, the displaced, the weak, and the marginalized. Ask him to help you come up with pro-active solutions to address the issues you are passionate about.

PRAYER

Jesus, guide my anger into appropriate action that reflects your love. Help me to honor you through all that I do. Amen.

LOVE ALWAYS TRIUMPHS OVER ANGER

The blind and the lame came to him in the temple, and he cured them.
(Matthew 21:14)

Regardless of Jesus' outburst in the temple, the blind and the lame were not afraid of him. Jesus may have driven out the cattle, the sheep, the doves, and thrown the money-changers' tables to the ground, but he did not turn away those who came for prayer and healing. His anger never triumphed over his love. He heard the cries of the blind and the lame, responded to their needs, and transformed their lives.

Notice that Jesus never tried to burden those in need with his anger. He did not discuss with them——or try to justify to them——the cause of his anger. He simply met them at the point of their need.

Sometimes our anger about "big" injustices can blind us to the needs right in front of us. We can become so immersed in our justifiable sense of what is right and wrong on a large scale that we forget we are called to care about the individuals in our daily lives who need our love. We might be so embroiled in the subject of our anger that we are oblivious to the physical or emotional needs of those around us.

In the face of injustice, it is appropriate to feel anger. Yet while Jesus experienced anger, he did not wallow in it. When he saw the temple desecrated by traders, he did not forget the neediness of his people. He always continued to love and to heal and to forgive.

Whatever you are angry about, ask Jesus to help you continue to love. Ask him to help you keep love at the forefront. Do not burden those in need of healing with your struggles with anger. Instead, welcome them and ask Jesus to help you be a vessel of his healing love.

PRAYER

Jesus, help me to surrender my feelings of anger to you so I can serve others in love. Amen.

PRAY FOR WISDOM

When those who were around him saw what was coming, they asked, "LORD, should we strike with the sword?" Then one of them struck the slave of the high priest and cut off his right ear. (Luke 22:49-50)

The angry mob that descended on the Mount of Olives where Jesus had been praying were there to arrest him. Startled, the disciples asked Jesus, "LORD, should we strike with the sword?" We might commend them for asking Jesus the question before acting on their impulse, but apparently it did not occur to them to ask Jesus, "LORD, what do you want us to do?" There was no doubt in the disciples' minds that violence should be met with violence.

But before Jesus could answer, one of the disciples cut off the right ear of the slave of the high priest.

As you read this, you might be wondering how this relates to you. You might not resort to physical violence, but have you ever had the impulse to take matters into your hands before you thought to ask Jesus how you should handle your predicament? Has your anger ever lit a fuse within you that made you want to fight fire with fire? Have you used words to destroy somebody's reputation or mar their character?

It takes discipline, and familiarity with Jesus' teachings, to learn how *not* to act out of anger. Be encouraged. Take counsel from Jesus' words and pray that when you are faced with contentious situations, you will make wise decisions *before* conflict surfaces.

And whatever you face, know that you are not alone. If you ask for Jesus' help with your response to anger, he will give it. Pray for Jesus' wisdom about what you should do. Listen to his assurance: "When they bring you before the synagogues, the rulers, and the authorities, do not worry about how you are to defend yourselves or what you are to say; for the Holy Spirit will teach you at that very hour what you ought to say" (Luke 12:11-12).

PRAYER

Jesus, help me to seek out your wisdom and heed your teachings before I react to conflict. Amen.

"NO MORE OF THIS!"

But Jesus said, "No more of this!" And he touched his ear and healed him.
(Luke 22:51)

As soon as one of his disciples physically harmed someone, Jesus put an end to the violence: "No more of this!" His words were sparse and concise, and he immediately healed the man whose ear had been cut off.

This time, Jesus was angry at the violence. But rather than staying focused on the deed, he moved quickly to a place of healing and reconciliation. Jesus chose neither the side of his disciples nor the chief priests and elders. Instead, he chose the side of God by loving rather than hating his enemies. What a marvelous example of how to defuse anger.

Then he turned to those who had conspired to persecute him and asked, "Have you come out with swords and clubs as if I were a bandit?" (Luke 22:52b). The crowd mentality was such that these leaders had allowed themselves to be swept away by each other's sentiments of ill will toward Jesus. Jesus did not condemn them, but his words called them to think about their actions and the methods they were employing to hurt him.

Anger, especially when fostered by others who share our anger, can easily become volatile and unbridled. Our feelings can be shaped and amplified by the sentiments of those around us. Have you ever found yourself in a situation where someone maintained a strong dislike for a friend, a relative, a colleague, and that dislike spread to the point where you, too, started treating someone you once thought of as a friend differently? It is easy to be swayed by the strong emotions of a crowd.

Perhaps you have allowed your feelings of anger to reach the point where you have physically or psychologically hurt someone. Take Jesus' words seriously: "No more of this!" Call on Jesus for forgiveness, and ask the people you have hurt to forgive you. Ask Jesus to heal you of harmful anger and to help you find new ways of dealing with this emotion.

PRAYER

Jesus, help me not to be led by the opinions and hateful actions of others. Forgive me for the hurt I have caused others and help me to reach out in reconciliation, healing, and forgiveness. Amen.

RESPOND RATHER THAN REACT

The scribes and the Pharisees brought a woman who had been caught in adultery; and making her stand before all of them, they said to him, "Teacher, this woman was caught in the very act of committing adultery. Now in the law Moses commanded us to stone such women. Now what do you say?" They said this to test him, so that they might have some charge to bring against him. Jesus bent down and wrote with his finger on the ground. (John 8:3-6)

They made her stand before all of them. They had caught her in adultery and dragged her before the crowd for everyone to stare at her. Now the scribes and Pharisees, who positioned themselves as gatekeepers of Jewish law, asked Jesus what to do with her.

You can almost hear the sarcasm in their question: "Now what do you say?" They called him "Teacher" as a mark of respect, but in actual fact they were using this woman to back him into an ethical corner. If Jesus did not approve stoning her, it would seem that he was breaking Jewish law, and they could bring charges against him. A kind of verbal battle of the minds ensued as Jesus' knowledge of scripture and Jewish law was being tested.

And what was Jesus' response? He did not take their bait by dazzling them with his stellar teaching. Instead, he did something quite curious. He bent down and wrote on the ground with his finger. It does not appear that the scribes and the Pharisees paid any attention to what he wrote. Nor does the Apostle John reveal the content of Jesus' composition in the ground. What we do know is that Jesus took his time to consider the best way to respond to their obvious mocking of his authority. He did not react out of anger but out of careful reflection. He did not allow the scribes' and Pharisees' verbal barrage and baited questions to shape his thoughts and actions. Instead, he took the time to compose his response.

When you are angry, you know how difficult it can be to step back from the situation and thoughtfully consider the best way to respond rather than react impulsively. To *react* would be to rely on your own initiative without bringing Jesus' teachings into the matter. To *respond*, as Jesus did, means taking time to apply Jesus' teachings to your actions. To

react would be to embrace the thoughts, motives, and behaviors of those who anger you. To *respond* means opening yourself to become a recipient of God's wisdom and a channel of God's love.

The next time you are in a situation where discord arises, take the time to prayerfully think before you speak and act. Ask Jesus how he would have you respond.

PRAYER

Jesus, teach me to respond to anger by looking to your wisdom for guidance and not to react to others out of a place of frustration or hate. Amen.

THE POWER OF REFLECTION

When they kept on questioning him, he straightened up and said to them, "Let anyone among you who is without sin be the first to throw a stone at her." And once again he bent down and wrote on the ground. When they heard it, they went away, one by one, beginning with the elders; and Jesus was left alone with the woman standing before him. (John 8:7-9)

Before long, Jesus straightened up from his bent position and responded to the scribes' and Pharisees' taunting question. His words were simple and relevant: "Let anyone among you who is without sin be the first to throw a stone at her." His words were not cryptic nor meant to baffle his audience. Instead, Jesus offered them a simple solution that did not feed into their verbal trap, nor enflame their anger further.

He did not wait for their reaction or try to goad them into a response, but stooped once again and started writing. His silent posture embodied the phrase "actions speak louder than words," and for a while he resisted speaking any further into the situation.

Scripture tells us that those gathered around him "heard it," but what did they hear? Did the sounds of Jesus' finger scraping the ground speak a language of conviction? In the silence, it was as if they could finally hear the truth of what he had spoken, and his words resonated deep within them. They did not utter a word but, one by one, starting with the elders, they departed from the scene, leaving Jesus alone with the woman.

Have you ever felt angry enough to hurl a "stone" of condemnation? Perhaps it was at someone who did not live up to your expectations, or at someone whose actions greatly disappointed you, or at a group of people who blocked something you were trying to accomplish.

The power of Jesus' example lies in his invitation to reflection. Jesus can step into the middle of your anger and steer you to reflect on your own shortcomings. His compassion can allay your impulsive anger that wants to lash out, and help you think about how your own conduct has harmed others—or yourself. He will not condemn you but cause you to deeply contemplate your conduct and the way you live your life. So when you find yourself ready to throw the first "stone," ask Jesus to probe your

heart and help you consider your own sins, even as you evaluate the reasons behind your anger toward someone else.

PRAYER

Jesus, help me to know when my opinions and actions do not reflect your love. Teach me how to surrender my anger to you. Help me to love as you love. Amen.

BEYOND BITTERNESS

Jesus straightened up and said to her, "Woman, where are they? Has no one condemned you?" She said, "No one, sir." And Jesus said, "Neither do I condemn you. Go your way, and from now on do not sin again." (John 8:10-11)

After the woman's accusers dispersed, Jesus rose from the ground and turned to her and asked, "Woman, where are they? Has no one condemned you?" This is the first indication that anyone actually conversed with her. Jesus did not talk at her, but to her, inviting her into a dialogue, and in doing so he conveyed her worth, no matter what she had done.

Her response to his questions was a simple one: "No one, sir." She must have been amazed to see the people leave without saying anything to her. Not one stone pierced her skin. In front of Jesus she stood, tall and upright, with not a bruise on her flesh. And in the midst of her awe, Jesus said to her, "Neither do I condemn you. Go your way, and from now on do not sin again."

In essence, Jesus told her to leave this place and mindset of condemnation behind her and walk in the freedom of knowing that he did not judge her. While Jesus recognized that she had sinned, his love instructed her not to sin again, and these words opened a new path of life for her.

This woman could have nurtured anger in her heart toward all those who had judged and shamed her and tried to abuse her in public. Alternately, she could have submerged herself in guilt about her past or been concerned about those who may not welcome this new change in her life. But she accepted the words and perspective of Jesus. She did not deny that she had sinned, but took responsibility for her past and moved on. Jesus' words released her from living out her life in anger.

Have you ever been in a position where you were judged in a public way? Have you felt bitter, angry, or resentful at the way you were treated? Will you allow Jesus' words "neither do I condemn you" to begin your healing? Will you choose not to be angry with yourself when you sin and, instead, ask Jesus to forgive you and transform you? Let Jesus release you from your anger and help you to move on.

PRAYER

Jesus, thank you for being sensitive to the moments when others have judged me harshly. Thank you that you listen to my cries when I am hurt or criticized. Help me not to be bitter, but to turn these feelings over to you. Lead me by the light of your words so I can move beyond my anger. Amen.

WORDS OF HEALING

"You have heard that is was said to those of ancient time, 'You shall not murder'; and 'whoever murders shall be liable to judgment.' But I say to you that if you are angry with a brother or sister, you will be liable to judgment; and if you insult a brother or sister, you will liable to the council; and if you say, 'You fool,' you will be liable to hell of fire." (Matthew 5:21-22)

Jesus spoke some pretty strong words. While his teaching about judgment may seem difficult or harsh, one thing is clear: Jesus was serious about the destructive nature of anger. When we allow our anger to fester and shape our actions, we will be judged.

But Jesus was talking about more than angry exploits; he was talking about the power of angry words. Their ripple effect can have a lasting influence on our relationships with others. Fighting within families can dismantle relational bonds. Insults to a brother or sister—either to a sibling or to those we think of as a brother or sister—can cause great damage. Calling someone names, using angry words, can be like taking a weapon and wounding their feelings—even maiming their character. How we talk about people can become a form of character assassination that can kill their sense of well-being. Angry words can even distort *other* people's perceptions of a person and cause them to ridicule or ostracize this individual.

The book of Proverbs conveys numerous words of wisdom about the significance and power of words:

Rash words are like sword thrusts, but the tongue of the wise brings healing. (Proverbs 12:18)

Those who guard their mouths preserve their lives; those who open wide their lips come to ruin. (Proverbs 13:3)

A soft answer turns away wrath, but a harsh word stirs up anger. (Proverbs 15:1)

It is wise counsel to be prudent with words. If you are quick to speak out of anger, if you are prone to tearing down people's self-esteem rather

than building them up, Jesus wants you to choose another way of communicating and relating. Are you willing to let Jesus reveal how your words can hurt others?

PRAYER

Jesus, help me speak words of healing rather than words of hurt. Amen.

MOB MENTALITY

Then the high priest tore his clothes and said, "He has blasphemed! Why do we still need witnesses? You have now heard his blasphemy. What is your verdict?" They answered, "He deserves death." Then they spat in his face and struck him; and some slapped him, saying "Prophesy to us, you Messiah! Who is it that struck you?" (Matthew 26:65-68)

When the crowd of scribes and religious leaders tried to goad Jesus into admitting that he was the Messiah, Jesus responded by saying, "You have said so. But I tell you, From now on you will see the Son of Man seated at the right hand of Power and coming on the clouds of heaven" (Matthew 26:63-64).

Their reaction was swift and brutal. The high priest tore Jesus' clothes and, with this single act, initiated a series of assaults on Jesus' character meant to humiliate and destroy him. No one in the crowd came to Jesus' defense. No one in the crowd opposed the brutal actions of those who claimed they were acting in the name of God. And Jesus did not utter a word.

Anger thrives off the disgruntlement and despondency of others. Anger mocks. Anger chides. Anger enforces a particular worldview, a particular agenda, a group mentality. It is not uncommon to find this kind of "mob mentality" in various areas of our lives. The workplace, church, family gatherings, college, school, sports arenas can all be breeding grounds for group anger to flourish.

Have you ever found yourself participating in such a group or crowd, perpetuating or even escalating anger? If you have seen this behavior in yourself, ask for Jesus' forgiveness and ask him to help you identify the source of your anger. Ask for healing from this anger.

Choosing not to respond to an angry mob mentality requires Jesus' strength. It is Jesus' might that will keep you from being swept away by the heated emotions of a group. It is Jesus' wisdom that will show you how to respond to such behaviors. And it is Jesus' power that will give you the courage to do the right thing and stand up for justice when it is required.

PRAYER

Jesus, sometimes I am afraid to challenge those whose opinions and convictions dominate the circles I move within. I confess it is often easier to be quiet and not say a word when others speak words of ill will. Help me not to surrender to this "mob mentality" but to follow your lead and be an advocate of your justice. Amen.

A PLACE OF FATIGUE

In the morning, when he returned to the city, he was hungry. And seeing a fig tree by the side of the road, he went to it and found nothing at all on it but leaves. Then he said to it, "May no fruit ever come from you again!" And the fig tree withered at once." (Matthew 21:18-19)

Jesus was hungry. He had traveled on rugged terrain from Jerusalem, returned to Bethany for one night, and then had made his way back to Jerusalem. Traveling such long distances in such a short space of time would have been arduous. And perhaps the everyday demands of his ministry kept Jesus from giving much thought to what he would eat. Given his fatigue, perhaps seeing the barren fig tree was the last straw. In any case, Jesus took out his frustration on the tree: "May no fruit ever come from you again!"

When we are weary or hungry or have not slept well, we are much more susceptible to irritation and anger. Who or what do you take your anger out on when you are frustrated? When are you most likely to become irritable? Knowing the situations that can spark your anger is a good place to start when you ask Jesus to help you change your behavior. For instance, if you are not a "morning person," you might take out your disgruntlement in the morning on those closest to you. Ask Jesus to help you better communicate your feelings so your words and actions do not hurt others.

However, no matter how well you understand the triggers that provoke your anger, an unexpected event can bring on a force of anger that you were not prepared to feel and cause you to strike out quickly. When this happens, seek forgiveness from those who have borne the brunt of your anger. And ask Jesus to help you transcend your feelings of impulsive anger.

PRAYER

Jesus, help me to come before you when I am feeling irritable. And help me to be mindful of taking care of myself so that I do not take my anger out on others. Amen.

FRUIT OF ANGER

When the disciples saw it, they were amazed, saying, "How did the fig tree wither at once?" Jesus answered them, "Truly I tell you, if you have faith and do not doubt, not only will you do what has been done to the fig tree, but even if you say to this mountain, 'Be lifted up and thrown into the sea,' it will be done. Whatever you ask for in prayer with faith, you will receive." (Matthew 21:20-22)

While some may question the wisdom of Jesus cursing a fig tree, the lesson he taught from this incident is one of ongoing faith.

Take another look at Jesus' example. Jesus may have been hungry and taken his frustration out on the fig tree, but his faith in God never diminished. Which is why Jesus used this moment as an opportunity to teach his disciples about the power of prayer. This may seem like an odd shift in intention, but out of the death of a fig tree Jesus could instruct his disciples about the life-giving properties of prayer.

When the disciples looked at the withered fig tree, they saw something barren, but Jesus turned their perspective toward the power of faith. Similarly, when we are confronted with the results of our anger, we have an opportunity to turn to faith.

If you find yourself preoccupied with anger, ask Jesus to help you refocus on his power. This is essential if you are to live out a life ruled less by anger and defined more by hope, because anger can quickly cast a dismal perspective on the present and future. Ask Jesus to help you to remember what God can do in your life and the lives of others, and allow Jesus to transform your anger into faith. And do not settle in your prayers for small results, but pray big and far and wide. Pray for the impossible because no matter what anger you feel about the situation you face, Jesus can make the impossible happen.

PRAYER

Jesus, remind me again and again that you can perform miraculous deeds. Help me not to allow anger to deplete my faith in you. Amen.

RECONCILIATION

*So when you are offering your gift at the altar, if you remember that your
brother or sister has something against you, leave your gift there before the altar
and go; first be reconciled to your brother or sister, and then come and offer your
gift." (Matthew 5:23-24)*

Jesus was serious about reconciliation. He went so far as to say that,
before we bring our gifts "to the altar," we should stop everything and do
what we can to make things right.

Reconciliation is not easy. At times it seems easier to avoid someone
you have hurt because facing up to the ways you have wounded them may
be too difficult. You may still be struggling with your anger, or you may
fear their anger toward you. The irony is that the longer you keep away
from the person you have hurt, the more time they have for their anger
to build.

Jesus calls you to be an ambassador of reconciliation. Start by recognizing that you are reconciled to God through Jesus. Receive the forgiveness of Jesus, and with this acceptance, ask him to turn your behavior into
a healing balm. Give your anger to Jesus and ask him to help you discern
the best action to take. Jesus can help you find the words of reconciliation to speak. Ask him to help you take ownership of your behavior. Ask
him how he wants you to make amends for the ways your anger has hurt
others. Depend on him to help you demonstrate his love as you seek their
forgiveness.

And if the person you have hurt does not accept your desire to seek
their forgiveness, do not become despondent or more angry with them
for rebuffing your attempts to resolve the conflict. Whatever the outcome, you—and the one you have hurt—will always be embraced by
Jesus' love. Continue in prayer, and continue in your efforts to demonstrate this love.

PRAYER

*Jesus, reveal to me the ways in which my words and actions have hurt others and
show me how to reconcile with those I have hurt in anger. Amen.*

MANAGING ANGER

The following guidelines offer some ideas about ways to manage your anger. Whatever strategies you decide to employ, ask Jesus to guide you in implementing them in your life. Look for guidance in his wisdom and permit him to lead you into a life of peace.

1. Jesus can handle your anger. Don't be afraid to tell Jesus exactly what it is on your mind.

Jesus wants to hear the reasons why you are angry. Even if you are angry with Jesus, he wants to know that, too. It can be a healing experience to know that Jesus' love will not be drained by your anger, that he will not try to silence you when you communicate your anger to him. He will sit with you in your anger and give you relief from this emotion. As scripture teaches, "One who is cool in spirit has understanding" (Proverbs 17:27b).

2. Praising God soothes the anger away. Praising God in the midst of your anger may seem odd, and even strained, but in praising God you can hold onto the hope that Jesus' love can transform your anger and enable you to be a bearer of his compassion.

When anger touches you, give God your thoughts and feelings. One of the profound blessings of praising God is that it envelops you in God's desire to reconcile his people to himself, through his son Jesus Christ. God brings joy to all those who seek to glorify his name, even when we are angry with him and take issue with his teachings (see Psalm 43:1-5).

Praising God can help you shake off the feelings of despondency framing you, and it can temper your disgruntled mood. You might find it helpful to listen to music that focuses on the glory of God, or sing praise songs. You can ask God to replenish your mind with thoughts of God as a provider, as someone who is willing to partner you in whatever trial you face.

Picturing Jesus caring for you, and visualizing Jesus listening to you as you talk to him, can assure you that Jesus is ever present to your concerns. If your anger persists, ask God to give you his peace.

Be encouraged by the words of the Psalmist:

Why are you cast down, O my soul
and why are you disquieted within me?
Hope in God; for I shall again praise him,
my help and my God. (Psalm 43:5)

3. Ask Jesus for perspective. *Making significant decisions when you are angry can exacerbate the problems confronting you.*

Anger can narrow your viewpoint. When you are angry, perhaps the last thing you want to hear is what someone else thinks, what other factors need to be considered—even what Jesus has to say about the situation. Sometimes the hardest thing to do is to see the person or persons you are angry with in a new way. Your anger can blind you to seeing other dimensions of their character. Your anger can reduce that person or persons to a stereotype and dismiss them as less than human. At that point, you will stop seeing them as God's beloved, deserving to be treated as God's child.

Ask Jesus to help you surrender your lack of understanding to his wisdom. Let him teach you how to look at people and incidents from his broader perspective. Ask Jesus to help you see those with whom you are angry, through his eyes. Ask him for the perspective to appreciate their multifaceted character. With Jesus' help, you can view the object of your anger through his eyes of love.

From now on, therefore, we regard no one from a human point of view; even though we once knew Christ from a human point of view, we know him no longer in that way. (2 Corinthians 5:16)

4. Engage in other activities. *A change of pace, taking time to be with other people and creating time for quiet prayer, can reduce the internal pressure of anger and restore your outlook.*

Think of the number of injustices that Jesus confronted in his culture: injustices affecting the poor, the widowed, the disenfranchised, the lonely, the broken-hearted, the sick, and the lame. Don't you think he might have been angered over some of the things he encountered? But this did not make him retreat from people. He always took time to socialize with people, and table fellowship was a central part of his ministry.

When you feel strongly about a particular injustice, or when your feelings of anger seem particularly overwhelming, you may place a low priority on participating in activities that would take your mind off your anger. Simple activities, such as going out to dinner with friends, playing board games, going for a walk, taking a drive into the countryside, or watching a movie can rejuvenate you and rebalance your feelings.

It was also Jesus' custom to create periods for prayer. He made it a priority to get away for some quiet moments with his heavenly Father. Spending time with Jesus does not have to be limited to verbal prayer. Consider inviting Jesus to take a walk with you, to sit by you as you garden, to come along on your next fishing trip. Use your encounters with him to surrender your anger and experience his solace and comfort.

5. Be watchful that your answer doesn't turn into cynicism. If you find yourself in a position where your anger feels more important than what you are angry at or with, or if anger seems to be shadowing many aspects of your life, ask Jesus to help you sort out what is misplaced or misguided.

If you find yourself seeing only what is wrong in the world, it might be time to evaluate the usefulness of your anger. Anger can breed cynicism that blots out any semblance of hope or healthy partnership with others. Anger can also lead us to surround ourselves with people who agree with our perspective and will not encourage us to transcend these feelings for the common good of others. The challenge for all of us is to invite Jesus into those discussions and allow him to inform how we respond to any inequity. By permitting Jesus to guide how we should address wrongdoing, we open ourselves to the breadth of his teachings. When we submit to Jesus' leading, hope rather than cynicism will occupy our thoughts and actions.

Ask Jesus to help you envision the world through his eyes. This does not mean that you will not be disturbed or be moved to action by the various injustices you witness, or that your doubts and questions and anger will go away. But it does mean that Jesus will partner with you in a proactive faith that is defined by the wisdom of scripture. When you invite him into your thoughts, you will be less likely to be ruled or regulated by your feelings of anger.

Also, remember that when Jesus promised to feed the hungry, bring healing to the lame and the sick, he did not do this alone. He invited his disciples and other followers to join him in this mission. You do not have to stand alone in the face of injustice. Just as he called his disciples, Jesus calls you to love as he did. You can work with others to combat the issues of social justice as a community, joining together to replace anger with love, despair with hope. With this in mind, take some time to reflect on and be inspired by Jesus' words:

> "The Spirit of the LORD is upon me, because he has anointed me to bring good news to the poor. He has sent me to proclaim the release to the captives and recovery of sight to the blind, to let the oppressed go free, to proclaim the year of the Lord's favor." (Luke 4:18-19)

6. Consider how others can help. *If you are wrestling with managing your anger, or finding it difficult to identify the source of your anger, the help of a professional counselor can be helpful.*

If you feel that your anger is dominating your life, you may want to talk with a professional about how you can better manage this emotion. Sharing your struggles with someone or a group of trusted individuals who can support and encourage you while you learn how to manage your anger can be a tremendous help. Counseling can give you permission to be in touch with your anger, rather than running away from it or denying it, and help you come to terms with it. Counseling can also help you explore ways of expressing your anger that are not harmful.

You may also need healing for the ways you have been hurt by someone who acts out of their anger. In the face of their rage, you may feel silenced, dishonored, weak, or afraid. Counseling can equip you with the tools to deal with such individuals.

7. Practice a lifestyle of reconciliation. *Jesus calls you to be his ambassador and to share with others that they can be reconciled to God through his son Jesus Christ (2 Corinthians 5:20).*

Even when you experience anger, it is important that you do not lose sight of your mission to be an ambassador of reconciliation. Jesus calls you to be a living embodiment of his love to all you encounter.

If you take out your anger and frustration on those who are closest to you, consider the strain this behavior puts on these relationships. To cultivate healthy relationships that are guided by kindness and mutual respect, you will need to learn how to take charge of your anger so you do not emotionally hurt your closest companions, or take for granted those who are dear to you. Before greeting your family in the morning or evening, or seeing friends and colleagues during the day, give God your anger so they don't have to bear the brunt of your dissatisfaction.

Taking time to reflect on scripture is an important tool in learning new ways of dealing with anger. Ask Jesus to teach you his way of engaging with others. To start with, you might simply set aside five minutes a day to read scripture and pray. Or you might join a Bible study group that can partner with you as you seek to apply the words of scripture to your life. Other people can offer encouragement and share their insights that will enrich your experience of scripture. Ask Jesus to bring you to the point where you will desire to spend longer times reflecting on God's word, so that your knowledge of God's faithfulness and wisdom will deepen and bear fruit as you live out the call on your life as an ambassador of reconciliation.

As you read and study the Word, ask Jesus to teach you new ways of interacting that will enable you to transcend your anger and minister out of love.

All this is from God, who reconciled us to himself through Christ, and has given us the ministry of reconciliation; that is, in Christ God was reconciling the world to himself, not counting their trespasses against them, and entrusting the message of reconciliation to us. (2 Corinthians 5:18-19)

My prayer for you: I pray that you will not be ashamed of your anger or feel guilty or try to hide or suppress this emotion. I pray that Jesus will guide you to others who can help you address those areas of injustice that touch your heart. And I pray that your life will help others know that God, through his son Jesus Christ, is a God of justice and love. Amen.

7. UNFORGIVENESS

She became a parody of herself. She had devoted most of her adult life to being a dutiful wife and caring mother. She married her husband before graduating from college and gave birth to their first child a year after. Three children later, she cultivated a busy life as a full-time wife and mother. She took great pride in her ability as a gracious host. When her husband needed to curry the favor of his bosses, she organized tasteful evenings of culinary delights. When her husband enjoyed professional success and made frequent business trips, she managed the household chores and bills without complaining. When her husband got a promotion and they relocated to other parts of the country, she researched the new schools, called the movers, and oversaw the packing.

Sure, sometimes she and her husband argued. What couple doesn't? They quarreled about the amount of time he spent away from home. And yes, she grew frustrated about the little time he devoted to the children. In the quiet moments of her day, she sometimes felt underappreciated, and unloved, but she believed they were life partners tied to the common goal of raising children in a safe, secure, and reasonably happy home.

Overall, she considered her husband a hard worker and great provider who loved his family. So when he contacted her through his lawyer and told her he was leaving her for another woman, she was stunned. But when she received in these same documents the news that this woman was going to give birth to her husband's child, she sat at the edge of her bed and doubled over in pain. Even though she could no longer conceive a child, her womb ached for the fetus lying in the body of this other woman.

When the divorce was finalized, she still found it difficult to accept that her marriage was over. Her husband had wronged her. He betrayed her. Deep within her soul, the words rejected, abandoned, and disposable became the reference points signaling her now-acquired belief in her worthlessness. And for this breakdown in her self-esteem, for the loss of

physical touch, for the deep sadness she carried, for the hours she held her children in her arms and tried to explain why Daddy left, for the moments when she faced the brunt of their anger, for the times she wept over a stove while cooking, for the times she cried until sleep overcame her grief. For all of these, she could not—would not—forgive him.

With every ounce of her body, she resented that her life could be viewed as a cliché. She had become the archetypal dutiful wife and mother whose career-minded husband left her for a younger woman. As the scorned woman, she could not forget, and she would not forgive. Bitterness occupied her heart, self-pity emerged as her companion, and forgiveness was as illusive as trying to grab an image in a mirror.

Being unwilling to forgive can breed bitterness. It can skew our perspective. We can start to judge others and paint them with the same brush of contempt and disapproval as we do those who have hurt us. We can become so imprisoned by these thoughts that we inflict emotional harm on ourselves.

Yet forgiving is not easy; sometimes it can be downright painful. We may feel that forgiving someone absolves them of the wrongs they have committed. It is hard to let go of this sentiment, especially when the person does not seem remorseful. Who will punish them for what they have done? Why are they smiling and getting on with their life when they have injured us so badly? Does forgiving someone mean forgetting what they have done?

And what about those who do not believe they have done anything wrong? Do we forgive them? And *when* should we forgive another person? Do we forgive others *before* they ask for our forgiveness? What if we find we can't forgive someone, even when they have apologized for their actions and tried to make amends for their wrongdoing?

And what if someone can't forgive us? Or what if we can't forgive ourselves, even if someone else is able to forgive us? We may be so used to wallowing in guilt that we have come to believe that we will never be good enough, worthy enough, deserving enough to be forgiven. This guilt can be compounded even further if we come from families or cultures where guilt and regret are imbedded.

The first step in dealing with these issues is to consider how Jesus forgives us for our sins. We have all been offered the gift of forgiveness for our mistakes, shortcomings, and flaws. Jesus' unconditional love, his loving kindness, his grace will guide us when we wrestle with unforgiveness.

Learning to forgive is not a one-time event and, thankfully, Jesus does not suggest that it will be. When Peter asked Jesus, "How often should I forgive? As many as seven times?" Jesus said to him, "Not seven times, but, I tell you, seventy-seven times" (Matthew 18:21b-22). He was not suggesting that we adhere to a specific number, but that we recognize we will face the issue of forgiveness again and again in our lifetime.

Learning to forgive is an ongoing process of discovery. When we are having a hard time forgiving those who have caused us distress, we come up against shades of our character that we were not aware of before. For example, we may have considered ourselves loving and kind but find that feelings of hate or anger take hold of us whenever we think of someone who has harmed us in some way. Jesus will not turn his back on us when we find it difficult to forgive others. He will be patient with us.

Learning to forgive is a humbling practice because, even though we may want to forgive others by following Jesus' teachings, sometimes it can take us time to forgive them. We eventually realize that we cannot truly forgive without the love, wisdom, and guidance of Jesus. Jesus' forgiveness reminds us that it is only by his love that we can truly forgive others.

Learning to forgive also nurtures our spiritual health and mental well-being. There is freedom in learning how to forgive: freedom from the bonds of bitterness, anger, and hatred; freedom to love—even those who have hurt us.

Ultimately, discovering how to forgive is a day-by-day, moment-by-moment exercise in faith, and each time we learn another aspect of forgiveness, we have one more opportunity to thank Jesus for his ultimate forgiveness.

Give yourself a few minutes to picture
this scene of a son's unforgiveness:

*"Because this brother of yours was dead and has come to life;
he was lost and has been found."(Luke 15:32b)*

"How *could* you? I have never disobeyed you. I have never brought shame upon your household. I have done everything you asked me to do. Everything. I have worked hard for you, tended your lands, taken care of your property and cattle, and managed your servants and not once have I complained. Not once.

"And now, now that son of yours comes waltzing in, and you plan a party for him! Have you forgotten that he left without saying good-bye? Has it escaped your attention that he did not have the decency to thank you for his inheritance? Are you not concerned that he squandered the money you gave him on prostitutes? When he gallivanted across the country, he did not try to make contact with you. Not once. He did what he wanted to do, when he wanted to it, and thought of no one but himself.

"I simply cannot understand why you are rewarding him. I, for one, refuse to forgive him. I mean it. Why should I, you, anyone forgive him?"

His father listens carefully and does not say a word until his son's words come to an end. He gently puts his hands on his son's shoulders and says, "Son, you are always with me, and all that is mine is yours" (Luke 15:31). Then he quietly adds, "Your brother was lost; he was as good as dead. Now he has come back to us, to life. We have to celebrate."

Silence seals the elder son's lips as his father's words prepare the ground of his heart. The seeds of love for forgiveness are planted, with the hope that the weeds of unforgiveness will wither and this elder son will "hear the word and accept it and bear fruit, thirty and sixty and a hundredfold" (Mark 4:20b).

THE PRELUDE TO FORGIVENESS

"I will get up and go to my father, and I will say to him, 'Father, I have sinned against heaven and before you; I am no longer worthy to be called your son; treat me like one of your hired hands.'"(Luke 15:18-19)

Jesus told the story of a man who had two sons. One day, the youngest son demanded that his father hand over the share of the property that would be bequeathed to him. His father did not question his son's demands, but divided up the property and gave both of his sons their inheritance. After receiving his father's gift, the youngest son gathered all he owned and journeyed "to a distant country, and there he squandered his property in dissolute living" (Luke 15:13b).

But his arrogance was brought down after he spent all his money. A brutal famine swept the country, and he found himself desperate for food and work, even to the point where he was willing to feed pigs. He who once had family, food, shelter, and clothing would now have been happy to eat what was given to the pigs. He was far from home, alone, and dying of hunger. Perhaps this is the way of sin. It often takes us emotionally, physically, and spiritually away from those who love us.

No one offered to help him. No one took pity on him. He had reached rock bottom. In this state of destitution he could have blamed others for his misfortune, since those who had helped him spend his money did not come to his aid when he was in dire need.

Instead, the young man realized how grievously he had sinned against his generous father. He also knew that his father's hired hands always had more than enough to eat. So he decided to return home, not presuming he could return as a son, but hoping his father would take him in as a hired hand. He was ready to ask his father's forgiveness with the humble words, "I have sinned against heaven and before you; I am no longer worthy to be called your son."

He was finally willing to take complete ownership of his actions. He did not try to make excuses for the poor choices he had made. His realization that he had sinned against his earthly father, and against God, was a far-reaching confession steeped in humility.

Humility is the prelude to forgiveness.

If you find yourself feeling distant from God, from those who love you, it is a signal that you need to consider the steps that have taken you so far away. Take some time in prayer to search your heart. Ask Jesus to help you see and understand the places where you have disconnected from God, from others——even from yourself. Pray for the humility to go to those from whom you need forgiveness.

PRAYER

Jesus, help me to know that I can never stray from the depths of your love. Teach me humility so I can draw closer to you and to those I love. Amen.

THE ARMS OF FORGIVENESS

So he set off and went to his father. But while he was still far off, his father saw him and was filled with compassion; he ran and put his arms around him and kissed him. Then the son said to him, "Father, I have sinned against heaven and before you; I am no longer worthy to be called your son." (Luke 15:20-21)

How many times had the father stood watching, hoping for his son to return? The day he saw his son in the distance, heading for home, he was instantly moved with compassion. Running with his arms open wide, he embraced his son and kissed him.

The young man stood before his father, spiritually and emotionally vulnerable. He had no expectation that his father would receive him into the family fold. He did not know whether his father would call him son. He felt undeserving of any form of compassion and considered himself unworthy of his father's love. As far as he was concerned, his only hope was that his father would employ him as a hired hand. He did not dare assume he could ask anything more.

Sometimes it is too hard to receive forgiveness. If you have wronged someone or disappointed them or distanced yourself from them, you might struggle to believe that they could embrace you with forgiveness. You might even have trouble believing that God wants to forgive you. Can you imagine God watching, hoping for your return? Can you imagine God standing with open arms, ready to hold you?

Maybe you are like the son—expecting the worst. Is there an area of your life hidden in the shadows that you are too ashamed to bring to Jesus? Take heart from this story and picture Jesus' joy at your return. Wherever you are in your faith journey, Jesus' love is always waiting for you. He is always eager to forgive you and shower you with his grace. His love will always celebrate your decision to abide in his love.

PRAYER

Jesus, I know you will always open your arms of forgiveness toward me. Thank you that, no matter what I have done, you are always eager to love me. Amen.

AMAZING GRACE

But the father said to his slaves, "Quickly, bring out a robe—the best one—and put it on him; put a ring on his finger and sandals on his feet. And get the fatted calf and kill it, and let us eat and celebrate; for this son of mine was dead and is alive again; he was lost and is found!" And they began to celebrate. (Luke 15:22-24)

When his son came back, notice what the father did not do: He did not press his son for details about his sins; he did not question, "Where have you been and what have you been doing all these years?" He did not express anger, or yell at his son for wasting the family money, or try to shame his son in any way. It was enough that his son had returned to him and was alive.

Upheld by the sheer joy of having his son back, the father turned to his servants and told them to dress his son in "the best" robe, place a ring on his finger, and bring sandals for his feet. They killed a fatted calf and everyone in the household enjoyed a feast together, celebrating this son's return. Joyfully, the father proclaimed, "This son of mine was dead and is alive again; he was lost and is found!"

The son may not have been physically dead, but his choices had led him into a life where he was numb to the love and forgiveness of God. But his father understood the amazing gift of grace. The father's extravagant forgiveness stemmed from the source—God's perfect and fathomless love.

Perhaps there is someone you don't think is deserving of your forgiveness. Perhaps you have grown weary of their behavior because they keep going back to the same habits they promised to renounce.

Or you may have a child who is distant from you, or a friend who has chosen to separate him- or herself from Jesus. Someone you care about may have squandered their life. How can you respond to them with love and forgiveness? Ask Jesus to help you let go of anger, of judgment, of any feelings of superiority you may hold. Ask Jesus to lead you to compassion for those who need your forgiveness.

PRAYER

Jesus, I once was lost but now am found. You never gave up on me. You did not turn your back on me. You did not see me as a lost cause. Jesus, I do not understand your amazing grace, but I am thankful. Teach me the depths of your compassion so I can extend your love to those whom I need to forgive. Amen.

FORGIVENESS GOES BEYOND "FAIR"

Now his elder son was in the field; and when he came and approached the house,
he heard music and dancing. He called one of the slaves and asked what was
going on. He replied, "Your brother has come, and your father has killed the fat-
ted calf, because he has got him back safe and sound." Then he became angry and
refused to go in. (Luke 15:25-28a)

There is another key person in this story: the elder son. This is the dutiful son who remained faithful to his father. This is the loyal son who did not squander his share of the property or leave his father to pursue his own life. He stayed at home to work in the fields and tended the family land. So when he made his way home one day and heard the music and jollity, and saw people dancing, the revelry puzzled him. But when he learned that his father had ordered the killing of a fatted calf in celebration of his younger brother's return, his curiosity turned to anger.

Perhaps he remembered the anguish his father had endured during the long years, not knowing the whereabouts of his younger son. Certainly, he resented the fact that he had worked for his father for many years, never disobeying him. He was deeply aware that his father had never ordered his servants to slaughter "even a young goat so that [he] might celebrate with [his] friends." In his tirade he announced, "But when this son of yours came back, who has devoured your property with prostitutes, you killed the fatted calf for him!" (Luke 15:29-30). Notice his language: He could not even bring himself to call his sibling "brother," but referred to him instead as "this son of yours."

After he poured out his anger, his father made a simple statement, tenderly calling him "son" and recognizing his loyalty. The father explained that this was a celebration "because this brother of yours was dead and has come to life; he was lost and has been found" (Luke 15:31-32).

Sometimes forgiveness does not seem fair. It may seem that those who are wayward and downright foolish in their actions are undeserving of forgiveness.

If you find yourself inwardly protesting the idea of forgiving someone, if you take issue with Jesus about his idea of forgiving everyone,

every time, talk with Jesus about it. Like the elder brother, you can express your resentment to Jesus, and he will listen. Ask Jesus to help you understand the source of your unforgiveness. You may not feel appreciated for the ways you have been faithful. You may resent the attention someone is getting when it appears they have not lived an exemplary life. Your unforgiveness may be a camouflage for the discontentment you are feeling about your own life.

Let Jesus reassure you of his love for you — and his joy at the return of another. He will not turn his back on your anger or disappointment. Let his expansive forgiveness also show you that there is nothing you could ever do to put yourself beyond the boundaries of his love.

PRAYER

Jesus, thank you that I can share my struggles with you about forgiveness. Amen.

JUDGMENT AND SELF-RIGHTEOUSNESS

Now when the Pharisee who had invited him saw it, he said to himself, "If this man were a prophet, he would have known who and what kind of woman this is who is touching him — that she is a sinner." (Luke 7:39)

When the Pharisee witnessed the woman repeatedly kissing Jesus' feet and washing them with her tears and ointment, he was repulsed. According to him, "this kind of woman" was not worthy to have contact with Jesus. The Pharisee's comments implied that anyone who interacted with her ran the risk of being tainted with the same brush of dismissal that marked her life. With the use of the word "sinner" to describe her, he belittled her actions and nullified her personhood. In his eyes, she was no one of significance. She was a sinner and no other explanation was needed.

That is the nature of unforgiveness. It cultivates a spirit of judgment. It demeans another person's character and falsely elevates our own sense of pride. When we label the behavior of others, it is a good indication that unforgiveness has spilled into a mindset of self-righteousness.

If you are finding it difficult to forgive someone, ask yourself these tough questions: Do you consider yourself to be a better person than they are? Do you present yourself in ways that make you seem more thoughtful, trustworthy, and upstanding than the one you need to forgive? Do you thrive on exposing the mistakes of another?

Ask Jesus to show you how you can rise above this mindset by first confessing your own sins. Ask Jesus to help you examine your heart and ask for his forgiveness that has no limits.

"O LORD, you have searched me and known me.
You know when I sit down and when I rise up;
you discern my thoughts from far away.
You search out my path and my lying down,
and are acquainted with all my ways." (Psalm 139:1-3)

PRAYER

Jesus, help me to recognize my propensity to judge others. Forgive me for belittling or criticizing people. Free me from the grip of judgment. Teach me that I don't have to gain my sense of worth from putting others down. Teach me to be content in experiencing my worth in you. Amen.

AN INVITATION TO INTROSPECTION

Jesus spoke up and said to him, "Simon, I have something to say to you." "Teacher," he replied, "speak." "A certain creditor had two debtors, one owed five hundred denarii, and the other fifty. When they could not pay, he canceled the debts for both of them. Now which of them will love him more?" Simon answered, "I suppose the one for whom he canceled the greater debt." And Jesus said to him, "You have judged rightly." (Luke 7:40-43)

The Pharisee's name was Simon, and Jesus had something to say to him. While Simon did not publicly air his disgruntlement about this woman, Jesus sensed his disapproval of her character. But rather than mimic Simon's behavior, he acknowledged Simon's worth by calling him by name. In doing so, Jesus modeled how he will respond to us when we grapple with unforgiveness. He will call us by name and invite us to enter into a time of introspection.

The story Jesus told Simon was classic: a creditor canceled debts for two people who owed him vastly different sums of money. Jesus invited Simon to think through the situation and consider its deeper meaning. Jesus made no distinction between which debtor's note was worthier of being forgiven. Both debts were canceled; both debtors were forgiven for managing their funds so poorly.

Ultimately, Jesus' aim was to challenge and transform Simon's judgmental thinking.

By asking him, "Now which of them will love him more?" Jesus was encouraging him to think critically and consider how the measure of forgiveness was related to the measure of love. When Simon answered that the greater love would come from the one with the most to be forgiven, do you suppose a light bulb went on in his head? Did he have an "aha" moment and realize that the "sinner" before him might be worthy of love——both of giving it and receiving it?

As you enter into a time of introspection, allow Jesus to teach you about the life-giving freedom of his love and forgiveness, and to reveal to you what he wants you to learn from this passage.

PRAYER

Jesus, thank you that you are my teacher. Help me to consider how my unforgiveness influences the way I treat others. Help me to live out the truth of your teachings, especially in this area of forgiveness that is so complex. Amen.

LOVE PRECEDES FORGIVENESS

Then turning toward the woman, he said to Simon, "Do you see this woman?"
(Luke 7:43b-44a)

As far as Simon was concerned, the woman's behavior and reputation defined her. To Simon, the woman was invisible, and he saw her through the eyes of judgment. But when Jesus looked at her, he saw a woman of value. Rather than counting her sins against her, or condemning her, or dismissing her, Jesus saw her through the eyes of love.

Unforgiveness encourages us to view the person or people who we refuse to forgive as stock characters. What we mostly see are their faults, their flaws, and the non-endearing features of their personalities.

While there is no evidence in this passage that Simon needed to forgive this woman, this portion of scripture does call our attention to how easy it is to reduce a person's humanity to a global generalization—especially if we are struggling to forgive them for a real (or imagined) abuse.

What do you see about the person or people who have ill-treated you? Can you see only their harmful actions or hear only their scathing words? And what about those whom you disapprove of? Do you see their flaws? Do you see their shortcomings? Do you find that every time you think of that person, the only emotions you feel are anger, disgust, or even hate? Whether you feel justified in holding onto your unforgiveness, or are struggling with being able to forgive, one of the ways you can invite Jesus to help you is to ask him to teach you how to see those who have hurt you or offended you through his lens of love.

Learning to love is inextricably bound with forgiveness. While you may intellectually know this, you may grapple with how to apply this teaching to your life. Don't put pressure on yourself if you find this hard to do at first. When you see an image in your mind that reminds you of why you hold onto unforgiveness, when the sight of someone or the sound of their voice triggers painful memories, ask Jesus to teach you how to respond to them with his love.

PRAYER

Jesus, thank you for your unconditional love. Teach me how to look at other people through your eyes of love. Help me be open to your guidance on how to show that love to others. Amen.

"GO IN PEACE"

"I entered your house; you gave me no water for my feet, but she has bathed my feet with her tears and dried them with her hair. You gave me no kiss, but from the time I came in she has not stopped kissing my feet. You did not anoint my head with oil, but she has anointed my feet with ointment. Therefore, I tell you, her sins which were many, have been forgiven; hence she has shown great love. . . . Then he said to her, "Your sins are forgiven. . . .Your faith has saved you; go in peace." (Luke 7:44b-50)

What the woman had done, what the nature of her sins might have been, were completely forgiven in the fullness of Jesus' love. He liberated her from the behaviors that tied her to spiritual imprisonment.

Though his act of mercy would not stop others from judging her, or indulging in thoughts of ill will toward her, or touting their own self-righteousness, the only thing that mattered to this woman was Jesus' love for her. She chose not to listen to Jesus' critics or to demarcate her existence based on other people's judgment. As she poured out her costly ointment, she did not put a price on love. Her faith in Jesus was absolute. With complete abandon, she entrusted her life and her love to him.

This woman could have nursed a spirit of unforgiveness toward those who tried to maim her character. She could have distanced herself from those who humiliated her in public or lived a life of distrust that robbed her of the emotional and spiritual freedom that comes with forgiveness.

Instead, she held onto a faith that Jesus' love and forgiveness was hers. And because she embraced the truth that she was God's beloved daughter, she no longer had to live a life ruled by anxiety and condemnation. Jesus affirmed her identity, and she was able to go and live in peace.

The wonder of Jesus' forgiveness is that it is not conditional and does not depend on what anyone else thinks or feels. Do you trust that Jesus' love is great enough to forgive you, no matter what is in your past? Ask Jesus to help you grasp the full freedom of his forgiveness. Until you are able to accept that, you will not be able to forgive yourself fully—or anyone else. Ask him to ground you in your identity as a child of God, free to go and live in peace.

PRAYER

Jesus, heal me of the criticisms that have caused me distress. Help me forgive those who continue to judge me and trust in your love. Help me to live a faith that celebrates your words "go in peace." Amen.

THE LINK BETWEEN FORGIVENESS AND UNFORGIVENESS

"Forgive, and you will be forgiven." (Luke 6:37b)

Jesus closed the Lord's Prayer with the following petition: "For if you forgive others their trespasses, your heavenly Father will also forgive you; but if you do not forgive others, neither will your Father forgive your trespasses" (Matthew 6:14-15).

Very simply, this tells us that our willingness to forgive others is linked to our acceptance that we are all sinners in need of Jesus' forgiveness.

Jesus always holds true to his promises. When he tells us to forgive others, he assures us that he will also forgive us for the trespasses we have committed. It is a clear statement that resonates with his loving mercy. But if we choose to reject his teachings, if we choose to foster unforgiveness in our hearts, we will deny ourselves the gift of being forgiven by Jesus.

Jesus knows that others will trespass against us, but he offers us a way of responding to those who have caused us pain: to forgive them. If you are to receive Jesus' wisdom on this matter, you need his strength and his guidance. You can ask Jesus to help you if you find that your unforgiveness has hardened your heart or turned to bitterness. You can cry out to Jesus and plead with him to help you understand why and how you should forgive. You can tell Jesus that his teaching perplexes you. Jesus is ever ready to share with you his fathomless wisdom.

Choose daily to come before him and let his love transform and free you from those sins and stresses related to unforgiveness.

PRAYER

Jesus, thank you that you desire to forgive me. And I thank you that by your strength and wisdom I can forgive others. Amen.

LACK OF COMPASSION

But that same slave, as he went out, came upon one of his fellow slaves who owed him a hundred denarii; and seizing him by the throat, he said, "Pay what you owe." Then his fellow slave fell down and pleaded with him, "Have patience with me, and I will pay you." But he refused; then he went and threw him into prison until he would pay the debt. (Matthew 18:28-30)

In this story Jesus compared the kingdom of heaven to a king who desired to "settle accounts with his slaves" (Matthew 18:23c). When a slave could not pay back the ten thousand talents he owed, the king gave the order for the slave to be sold, along with his family and all their possessions. In distress, the slave pleaded with the king to save him, and the king had compassion and "released him and forgave him the debt" (Matthew 18:27b). But when this same slave confronted a fellow slave who owed him a debt, his reaction was fierce and unmerciful. He grabbed the man by the throat, ignored his petition for mercy, and "threw him into prison."

At times we suffer from what can be called spiritual amnesia and, like the slave whose debt was forgiven, we can easily forget how often Jesus has forgiven us for our mistakes, and how often others have forgiven us for our shortcomings.

Put yourself in the position of the person whom you are unable to forgive, and consider how you would like to be treated. Ask Jesus to forgive you for clinging to a mindset of unforgiveness. Then ask him to provide you with opportunities to make amends for your behavior.

Finally, contemplate the following question presented by the king and permit these biblical words to transform your thinking on forgiveness: "Should you not have had mercy on your fellow [brother or sister], as I had mercy on you?" (Matthew 18:33).

PRAYER

Jesus, help me to make amends for the distress I have brought to other people's lives. Help me to show mercy to those who I think are undeserving of such kindness. Amen.

"SEVENTY-SEVEN TIMES"

Then Peter came and said to him, "Lord, if another member of the church sins against me, how often should I forgive? As many as seven times?" Jesus said to him, "Not seven times, but, I tell you, seventy-seven times." (Matthew 18:21-22)

Ever ready to be the bright one, Peter offered an answer to his own question before giving Jesus a chance to respond: "How often should I forgive? As many as seven times?" By multiplying Peter's assessment, Jesus clearly illustrated that forgiveness is not a one-time event.

While Jesus' teaching addresses forgiveness in general, Peter's request was specifically about "another member of the church." This points to the difficulty of forgiving those whom we hold to a higher standard of conduct because they are fellow Christians. If a person in the church hurts us, or if conflicts emerge in a church setting, we may especially wrestle with forgiveness. And this climate of unforgiveness can carry over to other relationships.

You may know all too well how many times you need to be forgiven, and you may have experienced forgiveness many times. But how willing are you to forgive someone else over and over again?

Perhaps you are afraid of being taken advantage of. Or you believe that others might think of you as a fool. Maybe you see forgiveness as a sign of weakness. Perhaps you feel you have to compromise your assertion that you were wronged. Or maybe you feel that the person you have to forgive is undeserving of such compassion. Before long, unforgiveness can seem easier and more legitimate.

Can anyone really forgive seventy-seven times? Do you know what keeps you from forgiving? As you ponder these questions, you will find that the only place where you can learn this kind of forgiveness is from Jesus. Without his assistance, practicing forgiveness is impossible.

Share your thoughts with Jesus. He can handle your misgivings about forgiveness. He knows you will face the issue of forgiveness many times in your life—as both the forgiver and the one who is forgiven. When you are overwhelmed by the prospect of forgiving others, he is there. His wisdom and love can help you let go of the pain someone has caused you,

and release you from your own burden of guilt. Tell Jesus exactly how you feel and ask him to help you integrate his teachings on forgiveness into your life. By doing so, you can become a living narrative of Jesus' reconciling love and forgiveness.

PRAYER

Jesus, thank you that forgiveness is not a one-time event. You are the only one who can teach me how to forgive seventy-seven times. Amen.

LEARNING TO FORGIVE

As you reflect on the following guidelines, ask Jesus to show you how you can forgive others and receive his forgiveness. Some of these strategies may be more useful to you than others. Ask Jesus to help you discern which lessons best apply to your situation.

1. Honesty is the best policy. *Be honest with Jesus about the matters troubling your heart.*

You do not have to deny your feelings in order to forgive someone. One of the wonderful aspects of Jesus' character is that he will never belittle your problems. You can go to him and share all that is on your mind with the confidence that he will listen carefully. Jesus will not be shocked by your sentiments or by the words you choose to convey your feelings. Sometimes you will need to empty yourself of these emotions before you can hear what Jesus wants to say to you. Also, do not be surprised if you find yourself discussing the situation at hand with Jesus on more than one occasion. Let these times of conversation remind you that Jesus will never be overwhelmed by the episodes you face.

> *"Let the little children come to me, and do not stop them; for it is to such as these that the kingdom of God belongs. Truly I tell you, whoever does not receive the kingdom of God as a little child will never enter it." (Luke 18:16b-17)*

2. Praise him in the process of learning how to forgive. *Praising Jesus can lighten the load of unforgiveness.*

Unforgiveness can burden us with bitterness. Our disgruntlement can foster a dismal view of others. Praising Jesus can elevate us from these downward emotions by occupying our hearts with an appreciation of Jesus' love and relentless desire to forgive all of our sins. Whether we sit on the ground, kneel, lie prostrate, stand up, raise our hands, shout out aloud, or silently lift words of adoration in his name, the most important thing is that we are reverencing Jesus through our praise.

When you seek to worship Jesus in the midst of your trials, you may feel like your attempts to revere him are contrived. You may even get

somewhat annoyed with Jesus if you feel your struggles with unforgiveness are still preoccupying your thoughts.

By asking Jesus to help you enter into a spirit of praise, you will begin to learn that praising God does not have to be dependent on how you feel. By proclaiming the authority of Jesus through worship and praise, you can be reminded that there is no trial that Jesus cannot help you overcome.

Listening to a Christian radio station or singing praise songs are ways you can drive out the affliction of unforgiveness from your life. These lyrical words of truth can remind you of God's word, his power, and unmatchable authority, and they can encourage you to direct your concerns to Jesus.

Ultimately, when you praise God you acknowledge his unsurpassable worth. You can praise God for the countless times he has forgiven you. There are many ways to praise God. You can praise him in the sanctuary (Psalm 150:1), outdoors, or in the city (Psalm 48:1-3, 46). You can dance (Psalm 149:3) or bow down (Psalm 95:6, 138:2) or leap in praise (Acts 3:8-9). You can take off your shoes and praise him humbly in your bare feet as a way of acknowledging his holiness (Acts 7:33). You can adore him in silent contemplation (Psalm 107:30). You can clap hands, shout for joy, and sing praises to God at the top of your voice (Psalm 47, Luke 19:37). You can read the Psalms or any segment of scripture as a form of praise (Psalm 119:129-132).

In time, the grip of unforgiveness will unravel, and a desire to forgive others will grow in your life as your own gratitude for the ways Jesus has forgiven you deepens and stirs your compassion for those whose actions you once deemed unforgivable.

3. Forgiveness and humility. *To admit that we do not know how to forgive, to accept our need for Jesus' help, takes humility. In those cases where you find it particularly difficult to forgive others, you might need some support. This is not a burden that you have to carry alone, but it takes humility to ask for help.*

Even Jesus needed his heavenly Father's help and guidance. Jesus testified to this when he shared in his teachings "Very truly, I tell you, the Son can do nothing on his own, but only what he sees the Father doing

. . . and he will show him greater works than these, so that you will be astonished" (John 5:19,20).

If you are feeling resistant about offering forgiveness, ask Jesus to lead you to a friend, a support group, fellow members of your church, a counselor, or church leader to partner with you. Jesus is more than able to guide you to trusted individuals who can uphold you in prayer as you learn to experience the gift of forgiveness in your life. This kind of assistance can bring tremendous healing as you seek to forgive others.

4. Forgiving is not the same as forgetting. *The challenge is not to latch onto the past, or to relive a hurtful episode, but to transcend these memories by allowing Jesus to guide you by his wisdom and not your hurts.*

Try as you might, you may find that, even though you feel as if you have forgiven someone who has mistreated you, you do not have the heart or the strength to forget what they have done. This may prove even more challenging if you see that person on a regular basis or hear their name being mentioned. Each time, you may be reminded of the ways they have harmed you. Jesus understands. Take heart. Jesus calls you to forgive those who have trespassed against you, but he does not command you to *forget* what happened to you. Ask Jesus to comfort you in the midst of your pain. As he listens to you, you will discover his patience and understanding as you grapple with this area of forgiveness (see Psalm 139:1-6).

Then ask Jesus to help you have compassion for the other person by understanding their perspective. You do not have to condone their choices, but you can have a better sense about why they made certain decisions and have chosen to conduct their life in a certain manner.

When memories of your ill-treatment come to mind, share with Jesus what is on your heart. There is not one event in your life that Jesus does not want to be a part of. He knows what you have experienced and will not dismiss your hurt. Jesus is not asking you to deny how others have harmed you, but he does want to take you to another level in your understanding of forgiveness. His love can heal your wounds, and his wisdom can help you envision and put into practice new ways of responding to old hurts.

5. What comes first, repentance or forgiveness? *Does someone have to take ownership of their actions before they deserve to be forgiven? What if the person or persons who have hurt you show no remorse for what they have done, or show no signs that they are in need of your forgiveness?*

Just as Jesus never makes anyone believe in him, in the same way you cannot make anyone admit to wrongdoing, show remorse, or see that they are in need of forgiveness. If you want to see someone pay for or take ownership of their actions, you will have to trust Jesus to administer the justice he sees fit to wield. As challenging as this may be, you will need to accept that, just as Jesus has given you the choice to heed the wisdom of his teachings, so he gives everyone the choice to accept or reject that they are in need of forgiveness.

Forgiveness should not be dependent on how another person is going to respond. Think of Jesus on the night of the Last Supper. He knew that his disciples would abandon him, that one of them would even betray him, but he loved them still. He did not wait for them to admit to wrongdoing before serving them the sacrament of remembrance (Matthew 26:26-30). Jesus was willing to forgive them even *before* they acted. Only God's love can offer that kind of forgiveness.

Perhaps one of the reasons why Jesus put so much emphasis on forgiveness is that he knows that healing is not only for the one being forgiven, but for the forgiver as well. When you can forgive someone—regardless of how they respond—your thoughts and actions will be less dictated by emotional pain. You will experience a cleansing and freedom that will release you to move on.

6. Remember your need to be forgiven. *Never forget that you are just as in need of forgiveness as the person who is the focus of your unforgiveness.*

As hard as it is to believe, Jesus will never count your trespasses against you. As you ponder scripture, notice that when he forgives someone, he does not present them with a long list of what they have done (Matthew 9:2-7). His words of forgiveness are often simple and to the point: "Take heart, son; your sins are forgiven" (Matthew 9:2c) or, "I tell you, her sins, which were many, have been forgiven; hence she has shown great love. But the one to whom little is forgiven, loves little" (Luke 7:47).

Asking Jesus to help you recall times when you received his forgiveness can help you to forgive others. Let these moments remind you that you are always in need of Jesus' mercy. Rejoice in this free gift of love that you do not have to earn.

> *"Do not judge, and you will not be judged; do not condemn, and you will not be condemned. Forgive, and you will be forgiven; give, and it will be given to you. A good measure, pressed down, shaken together, running over, will be put into your lap; for the measure you give will be the measure you get back."* (Luke 6:37-38)

7. Seeing through the eyes of Jesus' love. *Jesus can enable you to see the people who have caused you harm, through his lens of love. With his vision, you can experience freedom from the spiritually damaging effects of unforgiveness. Unforgiveness can cause you to see people only through the eyes of your pain. You might be able to see only their faults, their flaws, their abuses of you. You might replay the scenes of their mistreatment again and again in your mind.*

Jesus is not asking you to deny how others have harmed you, but he does desire to take you to another level in your understanding of forgiveness. He can soften your heart and restore your sense of spiritual well-being. First share with him the thoughts and feelings you harbor. Then ask him to help you see the person(s) who have hurt you through his eyes. Being able to forgive someone will emancipate you from the anguish, mental unease, and emotional pressure of unforgiveness.

Ask Jesus to help you live a life of love, not bitterness or hate.

> *He has rescued us from the power of darkness and transferred us into the kingdom of his beloved Son, in whom we have redemption, the forgiveness of sins.* (Colossians 1:13)

My prayer for you: No matter what state of mind you are in, I pray that you will know that Jesus wants to hear from you and that he understands your pain. As you learn to trust Jesus with your concerns, I pray you will be able to experience the liberating freedom of being able to forgive others. Amen.